D1167556

SONS *of* GRACE

mark hughes

Ten Tough Men Who Went From Hell to Happiness

ROCK REST PUBLISHING

© 2011 Mark Hughes
All Rights Reserved.

Edited by Sheldon Bermont & Mark Hughes

Rock Rest Publishing
P.O. Box 98
Swarthmore, PA 19081
www.SonsofGrace.org

ISBN: 978-0-9840383-0-5

Printed in the United States of America

Table of Contents

Foreword

Whether you're drawn to Mike Piazza's call for miracles, the glaring stare on the cover, or the tales of tough men, you're about to experience something incredible.

These stories represent many of us. They provide the gift of how to break through to "Yes, now IS the time for me." Each story is independent and can be read on its own, but you will find this extremely difficult to put down.

Although each guy in the book has had a tough, tortuous life, we've all traveled some of the same roads. Whether it be searching for answers, or crying out in despair. The writers beautifully articulate how they've felt, and give us great examples of transformation.

If you're looking for more peace and happiness in your life, turn the page.

—Eustace Mita Jr.

Introduction

It all started with a question.

By today's standards I was a pretty successful guy. But even with everything the almighty dollar can buy, I never quite figured out how to achieve peace. For the better part of it, my life was as far from peace as a man could be. So…every Friday morning I attempted to narrow the gap by meeting with a group of men, each searching for their own missing life ingredient. As I looked around the room, week after week, I couldn't help but notice a former Marine with a rack of tattoos, fierce crew cut, and been-there before look. I'm sure he observed my slightly gray, longish hair and demeanor no longer suited for corporate America. After putting my name together with a book I'd written, he took an entire year to approach me and ask, "Can I talk to you about your book, and about a book I'm thinking of writing?"

I told him, "I've been thinking about a book too, but on a completely different subject than my last one. I definitely have something to say, but there's not enough to fill an entire book…I've got enough for maybe one chapter."

He responded, "Well, I might be in the same boat…Not enough to say…because I've just started a new journey that's becoming the real story of my life. I just don't want to dwell on my former existence, although I know people would find it interesting."

Several cups of coffee later, we'd pulled back layers of the onion far enough to realize that although the details of our lives varied dramatically, we were a lot alike. He was a former Marine Sniper, now dealing with memories of a life once overflowing with rage, alcoholism, drug use, and suicide attempts. I was dealing with a giant dose of emotional baggage possessed by any self-inflated, over-driven successful corporate a—hole. The common denominator for us was our former desire to completely control

3

destiny on our own without help from anyone. We just handled our unquenchable thirst for control in different ways.

A few years ago you wouldn't consider inviting either one of us to your Christmas party. We were both textbook examples of men who had designed, and then proceeded to live, on their own self-destructive treadmills. This made us toxic to anyone we came in contact with. We went out of our way to completely ignore the signs along any road that could have ended of our anxieties – signs that could've directed us toward peace and happiness. We were intent on saying, "Not now" to any choice outside our narrow field of view.

After kicking it around for weeks, it came to us, that perhaps our message would be best delivered with the help of other story-tellers, each writing one chapter – each with decidedly different pasts and perspectives. Men like us, once extremely tough, racing at the speed of light, but going nowhere. Each of their stories would describe what had led to that pivotal moment when they were finally able to say, "Now...I'm ready now."

We started looking for men heavily burdened with ghosts in their closet, possibly men who lived on the wrong side of the law... even men who had lost all hope and considered ending it. The strange thing is, though, we didn't have to travel far to find them.

We found most of them right in our own backyard (our immediate community). Look around and you will see that look of quiet desperation in the guy at the gas station, the man waiting for the bus...the guy next to you at the bar...or in the mirror while shaving.

We eventually found ten men including ourselves: some through careful and patient research, and others by coincidence. Each man took their time to write his own chapter. Some were comfortable with the process; others struggled to get the words out. Within these pages, they candidly share the tonnage of havoc they once wreaked on this world. Tears were shed by most during their intense and introspective writing; recalling what made their lives, at one point, so different than the lives they lead today. And these were former murderers, mafia associates, college champion athletes…guys who, by their own definition of manhood, simply don't cry.

So with this…we collectively hope to let you know that peace inside your heart *is* attainable. Despite your addictions…despite your afflictions, there can be peace.

These ten brave men reached a turning point – sometimes decades late, but they got there just the same. They were able to acknowledge that they'd been lost, and with that acknowledgement came the strength to say, "OK, I'm ready **now**."

The journey begins.

The Motorcycle Gang Member

Ron Gruber

Son of Silence

For almost all of my life I'd been telling God to go straight to hell. I'm not referring to my choices along life's highway, or the assault, racketeering, and murder that I was charged with and definitely guilty of. No.....I'm referring to my personal philosophy that basically said, "To hell with you people and your so-called God and Jesus!"

As I write this, it stirs a strong memory of a murdered gang member who I rode with for over twenty years. I was in "the cold room," the place where dead bodies were drained of blood before they were buried. My brother lay there, cold and lifeless, with bullet holes in his head, back, and chest. I remember slowly combing his hair, knowing that what truly lay on this cold, stainless steel table was dead meat. The work of a--holes.

Every single time I was with a dead brother in the cold room, I had the habit of taking my hand and pressing down gently around the gunshot wounds as I talked to him as if he was still alive. This insane behavior seemed perfectly normal to me at the time. It seemed like some kind of ancient ritual a warrior would engage in after the battle, knowing that as a survivor he would be expected to fight again and again – to retaliate for his nation....retaliation against all enemies.

So, into the cold room walks an "Ozzy" looking couple (Ozzies are what we called the general public, like Ozzy and Harriet). They stood there staring at my blood-drained brother who was now being dressed. His colors were placed on him with pants, boots, knife, rings, and bit of blow. Some of our brothers were buried with their guns.

Then the Ozzy began to lecture me: insisting that *"their son"* not be buried looking like *that*. "His hair will be cut, face shaved, and he'll be buried in a suit!"

Ozzies don't understand they exist outside of our world. This Ozzy didn't realize that: not only was I the lead Enforcer in the Sons of Silence, but I was a 1%er (One Percenter) in the most dangerous chapter of the Sons—the Nomads. There are many false rumors as to what a 1%er truly is. I'll just say that 99.9% of people say they have done it, but they ain't done sh-t. I'm not trying to sound like a super bad-ass, because any true 1%er knows that a twelve year old can kill. I believe the true standard for the 1%er name is the ability to push through countless mind games and still show up for duty. Pushing through doubt and fear, and doing any "proper" thing you got to do--so people learn to stand down from you and your gang.

Not only did I hate myself at the time, but I didn't give a f-ck about these two squares who knew nothing about what mattered to their dead son laying there in front of them.

The Ozzy said, "He'll be buried Christian, because that's what God wants."

As my insides tightened with rage for this Ozzy and his f-cking God, I leaned forward and told him, "We need to get some fresh air." As I stormed outside, I struggled with the insanity of my death-ridden life.

Standing outside the building, in the middle of dozens of people, I pulled my 44 Magnum Smith & Wesson and proceeded to tell this fool, "Not only will our brother be buried just as he lived...but this [lifting my gun upwards and in front of his face] is God... the one and only true God! - the one that holds the power of life and death." Then I pointed the gun straight up and screamed, "Watch this!" as I fired four deafening rounds of 240 grain semi-jacketed hollow points into the sky.

As I lowered the gun, I thrust my face against his and through clenched teeth I hissed, "My god just shot your god, in the face! Right in his f-ckin face! What about it now!"

So how could a Nomad Enforcer in the Sons of Silence, a man who only existed to destroy and murder... a man who reveled in ultimate hatred, ever find solace in Jesus Christ? How could a man who not only said 'Not Now' to God, but 'Not F-cking ever' to God learn to give his soul, willingly and daily to God?

The answer isn't simple. But maybe my story can help someone out there.

◆　◆　◆

My name is Ron Gruber. I was born in Waterloo, Iowa. I am currently serving a 50-year sentence for second-degree murder. My mother would gladly tell you that I was hell ever since the day I was born. I was intent on hurting people, including my mother, before day one. It seems that I tried to enter this world sideways and every which way but right, until I finally found my way to the first scream of life.

I grew up on a fourteen-acre farm. We raised chickens, ducks, hogs, and dairy goats. Goats were our main farm animals.

I can't remember too many days my Dad and Mom didn't spend hating and fighting each other. My childhood dreams were mostly of growing up faster so I could put my Dad to sleep. Yes, put my Dad to sleep and escape his twisted version of fatherhood. I made my own choices to survive, not realizing that I was simply building my own prison. I became a man at war within himself.

I realized, at an early age, that my Dad didn't have the slightest affection for me or my brother, and he viewed my mother as nothing but property. He treated her as such, and my mother had been beaten down enough over the years to act the part.

I too existed not as a son, but as his property. Right from the beginning I was at war, a war that centered on my battle for freedom from mental and physical slavery. Our war was ugly and my father's primary goal was to destroy and shame me by designing twisted challenges for me to meet head-on, or receive the crown of a coward.

These constant, twisted challenges became an insane game of whether or not I was willing to risk all my chips, or wear that coward crown. You see, I had to learn right out of the gate that a coward will always stop short of crossing the line, allowing himself to think, "Don't do it…you might get hurt." For any normal person, this would be called a healthy survival instinct.

But beginning at seven, I had to learn that a winner forces himself beyond any common-sense fear to emerge victorious. To find the courage I needed to survive, I was forced to abandon normal understanding of good and evil and race into an unfeeling zone that the average man on the street knows nothing about and, hopefully, never will. That zone would become the major influence in the choices I made in life; both bad and, in the end, good.

The Games People Play

One of the head games my Dad would lay on me was downright brutal. Lying on the couch after supper, he would be eating from a can of mixed nuts and drinking his cold beer in front of the evening TV drone. Then during a commercial my Dad would ask me, "Do you want some nuts?" "Well do you?" The ball was now in my court because he knew that I knew what was coming.

I would walk over to get the nuts, and right about the time my hand got to the can, my Dad would grab my hand, and twist it around my back. Then he would hold both of my hands behind my back as if I was wearing handcuffs, put my head between his legs, cross his legs around my neck, and squeeze violently.

Gasping for air and choking, I would still try to fight him off with everything I had. And while he choked me with his legs, he would begin to beat my backside again and again. Sometimes he'd work up a fart just to add insult to his fun. I'd try to scream, but my windpipe was cut off. While I was crying like mad, he would just laugh and laugh. If I dared to avoid this sick game and say, "No, I don't want any nuts," then he would immediately respond with, "Come here! Come here I said!" And I'd have to stand there as he shouted me down like a marine drill sergeant, letting me know I was "nothing but a chicken-shit coward loser!"

I remember being seven years old and wanting nothing more in life than to do what other kids did with their Dad—play a game of catch – maybe just walk and talk. But the cards dealt to me were what they were. I was freakin' seven.

This father/son charade continued for three years and the constant label of "coward" enraged my heart to the point where I learned how to override my fear...the fear of that violent squeeze around my neck. I paid the price every time; and after a while he would simply throw me to the floor in disgust. But I would look him right back in the face, showing no pain. I had conditioned myself to take any amount of pain he could dish out to avoid being called a coward. No one would *ever* call me a coward. I didn't back down and that truly pissed him off. But, unfortunately, I had no idea he was just getting ready to up the ante.

It's strange how when you watch your parents fight nonstop; sooner or later you eventually land right in the middle of it.

I can still see my father, dead-dog drunk, with a cigarette hanging from his lips, eyes glazed, trying to explain again why he's hours late with the telltale lipstick of a strange woman on his clothes. All I could do was hate myself for not being able to break him into pieces, as he would begin to manhandle my mom.

She'd beg him to leave her alone, but that would just fire up his attack. I could hear her heart breaking with every cry for him to stop. He would try to justify cheating on her, in his twisted drunken state, telling her how "lucky she was to have a man who was willing to come home and even sleep with her fat, ugly, ass." In his mind, his actions were not to be questioned because what he did was all for his family no matter how it looked.

My heart couldn't take being tagged a coward another minute. I blurted out "Leave her alone Dad, leave Mom alone and get your hands off her!...Quit being mean to her again!" His immediate response was to grab me by the hair, slam me into the wall, and tell me to shut the f-ck up.

Mom yelled, "Merrill, leave him alone!" Everything began to spin. Then, as quickly as it started, it stopped. Like nothing had even happened, Dad stared out the window and said in a steady voice, "Marie, start heating up the water to pluck the chickens. We need 25 killed and cleaned by the weekend for the store. Since I won't get fed tonight, I might as well do the only thing I'm good for according to this household. That's work and bring in the money."

Mom said, "You're drunk Merrill...go to bed!" Dad ordered, "Do it now!" with the real threat of more violence in his voice. So Mom started heating the water while Dad stormed out the front door yelling, "Ron, you're the oldest. Get your ass out here and help me."

I looked into his drunken eyes and saw that telltale smirk on his face – that familiar knowing look that said, 'I challenge you boy. You a coward boy? What's it going to be?'

Dad took a pull from his Camel cigarette, followed by one from his beer and barked, "Pick a chicken and bring it to the chopping block...now hook his head between the two nails and hold 'em around the wings and shoulders and stretch that neck out real good."

Dad picked up the axe. "Now, you son of a bitch, you're the one always getting me and your mother into fights. I just hope that as upset as you've gotten me...I don't *accidentally* miss the chicken and hit your damn hand with this axe. Oh...that would be a mess!"

Naturally, my heart started to beat a mile a minute. I was scared to death and, at the same time, furious at myself because I knew my being scared was exactly what he wanted. I should have known this was coming so why couldn't I get used to it and be ready? Damn I hated myself almost as much as I hated him.

His face was twisted up in anger as he hefted the axe and let loose with a kind of sick growl as he prepared to swing. In my panic, the bird got loose and the axe hit the chicken's body instead of the neck. Its wings flapped like crazy while blood sprayed everywhere. With blood all over my face and shirt, I grabbed the dying chicken and wrestled him back on to the chopping block. I shut my eyes tight and hear Dad laugh as he swung the axe down again. When I opened my eyes again he started talking baby talk, "Is Ronny scared?"

24 more chickens to go; the nightmare was just starting.

It seemed like I was in slow motion as I stretched the next one across the block. My anger and fear took a turn this time. When he warned me again, in that taunting voice, that I might lose my hand; I looked up into his face and uttered in a low, lifeless, but rock-steady voice, "Do it....Do it, Dad....Do it."

The look he gave me at that moment will stay in my memory forever. We locked eyes, and the chicken's head was lopped off. As the blood spurted, I looked at the chicken and all I could think was "Damn coward...should have been a man about it."

I was barely 9 years old—and the evil of the very man I hated had begun to breed within me.

Here Kitty

We raised nearly 100 goats for milking and for show. Two goats named Kitty & Beauty were part of this herd. I watched them give birth to their kids; I watered them, milked them, loved them, and played with them. Hell, when you share five years of life with two friends that listen to you, you get attached.

Beauty was Mom's favorite. Mom would talk to her in front of us, and it seemed like Beauty knew exactly what Mom was saying. But because of this special attraction Mom had for her, there were times when Dad would, in the middle of an argument with Mom, walk to the pen, then beat and torment Beauty.

One day when my Mom was out getting groceries, Dad ordered me and my brother to get Kitty and Beauty and bring them to the gravel lot. We were told to set out a mixture of molasses and grain on the ground for them to eat.

Dad appeared at the back door with a 12-gauge pump shotgun. The shotgun had always bothered me, but at the same time, had always called to me as a symbol of power and respect. I said "I ain't watching you kill them, and I'm not going to help you with their bodies."

Dad walked up to me and said, "You will never grow up to be worth a sh-t. You'll never be a man. This is the way life is," and slapped me down to the ground. He jacked a round into the chamber of the shotgun and said, "You stand right there next to me and watch, damn it…and at least try to act like a man."

Kitty and Beauty were just three feet away from us. Happy as larks, eating the grain, and without a clue as to what the next few seconds would bring. Dad stroked the barrel of the shotgun, up and down on the center of Kitty's head. I closed my eyes and a thought flashed through my mind: Is Dad thinking of Mom right now as he's doing this?

"You open them damn eyes right now, you hear me! I said open them eyes and watch this you f-cking coward!"

I opened my eyes streaming with tears, and anger forced me to yell, "All right, do it, do iiiiit!"

The body kicks back. Her eye flies out of the socket, and blood shoots from her head with a bowl-sized hole in her skull. Fallen now, she begins to piss in the dirt. The second explosion to Kitty blows the jaw off her head. She tries to stand again, but the third explosion breaks her entire head into chunks.

My father………my father smiles at me and jeered, "Oh, is baby scared?"

I said to myself, 'We will see one day who survives this game.' But for some reason I'll probably never fully understand, I hated myself more than anything. I was 10 years old. The severe hatred between me and my Dad was deepening…becoming more dangerous by the day, forming a gaping wound inside my soul.

The Hate Replacement

I needed something to fill the giant void that day left inside me…to somehow prevent it from festering and getting bigger. We weren't allowed to have dogs at that time, so I wanted to buy one of the young kid goats as my own pet—buy it from my Dad.

But it was part of a larger plan. I would start my own herd, have my own farm, and be free from the man I called Dad…taking Mom with me. If the plan worked, better days would lie ahead.

The purchase price, however, for this young kid goat—was giving up my 50-cent weekly allowance for doing chores on the farm as long as it took to pay back (which would be never). Dad made sure I knew my entire allowance was going to him, and if there were extra chores, they were mine with no complaint. I agreed.

The three-day-old buck kid was my own, and I named him Chore Boy since that's how I got him. I could hardly sleep at night, wanting to climb in the pen the next morning to feed him. As days turned to weeks, and weeks to months, Chore Boy grew to know and love me. He followed me around the fields, laid in the grass with me; and I'd lay my head on his side and just talk. At times we even fell asleep side-by-side. We were inseparable. Chore Boy was my friend, and giving up my allowance, even being pushed to the limits with extra work, was a small price to pay for my new happiness.

School started and running home from school to let Chore Boy out of his pen and play became a ritual. But as I ran home from school one day, rounding the corner of the barn was a pile of something. As I drew closer I made out a pile of heads and guts of young goats. Dad had decided to butcher some of them for meat for this year. It was a sad time, but we lived on a farm and this was farm life.

But as I looked at the pile of guts and heads on my way to Chore Boy's pen, I suddenly froze. Half covered in intestines, blood, and waste--with his eyes closed and tongue hanging out, was the head of Chore Boy. I pulled his head out of the pile, brushed the guts and waste from his face with my hands...and then I exploded!

I began to scream, "Dad......you lied. You murderer! You f-cking bum, I'll kill you!" I can't remember if the words came out or if I just was screaming inside. But I knew that I wanted to kill him for my mother's sake, kill him for my brother, and for Chore Boy. At that moment my single purpose in life became to find the courage to kill this bastard.

I started running towards the house screaming, "Kill him!" I knew that I would be heard this time and the words would cost me the worst beating of my life. I was a slave to the anger and there was no turning back.

My Dad charged directly at me, his face contorted in hate, drew his belt from his pants, and proceeded to wave it in the air. He only needed one of his meathook hands to toss me to the ground like I was a rag doll. Between the belt blows, I cried, "You are a liar and a bum!" My only comfort was in knowing that I had at least made my stand for the only friend I had in life, the only source of happiness for an innocent 11-year old boy.

I was so empty. So confused. Soaked in anger.

Two months later we were eating evening supper at the dining room table. Mom passed the potatoes, then the corn, and then the meat. As I was halfway done eating the food on my plate, my Dad smiles at me and says, "Well, how does Chore Boy taste? You know you're eating him right now don't you?"

I spit the meat back on to the plate, but my dad grabbed me by the back of the neck, pushing my face down into the half-chewed meat on my plate, and ordered me to finish my food. As he let me go, after rubbing my face in the cooked body of my close friend, I felt a switch that seemed to flip in my brain. I had crossed some sacred line, never to return.

I looked him straight in the eye, proceeded to chew every piece of Chore Boy with my own sinister smile…staring at him the entire way. "Chore Boy's gone," I said, "Thank you for the supper. It was a very good supper. May I be excused now?"

As I gazed into my Dad's face that night, I saw something in his eyes I had never seen before. It was uncertainty. Yes, uncertainty of what he had created as a son. His reaction released a feeling of satisfaction in me like I'd never felt before. If you don't know how to kill your Dad at age eleven—this was the next best thing.

The battle for my soul was won. After four years of these twisted games, I leaped into the powerful arms of evil as my only means of conquering fear.

The Son No Longer...The Sons of Silence

When I turned thirteen, they finally divorced. Mom moved us to town, and though I was somewhat involved in sports, drinking and drugs got top billing. Down the street was the clubhouse of a motorcycle gang. I was enchanted by the deep-throated Harley Davidsons, the colors (membership patches), and the power and respect the gang members demanded. And, of course, there were the women; women who did whatever they were told, when they were told, and how they were told. These women were collected as property to trade or barter as each member saw fit.

Yeah, I was sure that I had found my new, true family. Within two years of being a "hang around" with the gang, my brother and I were allowed to prospect (the means of becoming a member of the gang) at the ages of sixteen and seventeen. The young age violated their own minimum of 21, but our hard hearts, strong fists, and fearlessness broke all the rules. I knew I had found my reason for living: power, violence, and sex.

I became a security measure known as an Enforcer at the age of 18. At 20, though, I began serving six years in prison, mostly at the Iowa State Penitentiary. Inside I became increasingly violent, dark and treacherous as each year of my six-year sentence wore on. I maintained a position in a prison gang, and my violence led me to serve numerous stretches in solitary confinement (a.k.a. the bucket) sometimes as long as 600-800 days. This was for numerous stabbings, a terrible beating of a guard, and other offenses. I was by no means the most dangerous inmate in the State Penitentiary, but I was known to deliver on any task asked of me by the prison gang, who we called 'family.'

The first year out of prison was the longest run I ever had at remaining free out in the 'real world.' Despite the parole regulations, I kept in touch with my gang. While I was fighting for survival, locked inside the system, my brothers on the outside had been busy. The gang hadn't been idle. They had made major moves to increase their power. The profit stakes had gotten higher, causing gang wars to rage out of control.

As I look back, I never even gave myself a chance toward freedom from gang mentality, or freedom from satan's ever-present temptation. Self-centered, self-absorbed (whatever the shrinks call it), I couldn't wait to return to the Sons of Silence, and the false illusion of power. I went back to the money I made by beating people up, the drugs, the strippers...the whole nine yards. And, I was profiting from all of it.

Only seven people are allowed, at any one time, to be in the Nomad chapter of the Sons. I was one of the seven, and I was a Nomad Enforcer—head of security at a national level. If my prior years in the Sons and prison weren't enough, the next few years as the Nomad Enforcer got even more violent, driving me deeper into drugs, sex, and violence. It was during this period that I committed murder for the first time.

As it says in the Bible...you will reap what you sow. Not only did I inflict pain, destruction, and murder...I got it back as I was shot, stabbed, run-over, and actually took a lot more beatings than I dished out.

I ran with men who went on crazy sh-t jobs. When you ride into town and stroll into a bar—you are ten feet tall and bullet-proof because you know that nobody's going to even think about f-cking with you. Occasionally someone will try to mess with you, but Nomads are different. Those seven Nomads are known to have killed and maimed — the best of the worst, but we got results and demanded respect in our world.

We would show up day or night, when least expected, and started destroying whatever and whoever stood in our way. There was only one sure future for the men I ran with: death or prison. And I'm here to tell you that prison, for most men, is just another form of death.

But in my fourth year as the Nomad's Enforcer, I hit a wall. That year, three of the seven Nomads took their own lives. The pressure we chose to live with day after day was more than enough to disintegrate the strongest man. One of the three took his life right in front of me, and he was one of the toughest men of all the 1%er's I had ever run with. He got right up in my face that day (I'll never forget it) and said, "I'm going to the f-cking dead chapter to be with the brothers who count...I can understand them! I know you love me." And just two inches from me, he pulled the trigger and shot himself in the head, his brain matter and blood spattering my cheeks.

That was the turning point. I couldn't see any reason to go on living the lie. My heart finally rejected all that senseless death and destruction. Just from habit, I kept the mask on for a while thinking that my brother who'd pulled the trigger had copped out. "After all," that old voice was taunting, "we know that true soldiers don't kill themselves and don't go out like that...hell, that's a coward's move." But in my heart I knew these men weren't cowards, I had seen them walk into sh-t storms that any sane man wouldn't consider for a half a second. So, after serving as a gang member for over twenty years, I took it to the bosses and announced my retirement. Or, as they called it, I was retarded.

Maybe Now

I settled in Kentucky, sold my bike, bought 80 acres with a broke down old farmhouse infested with raccoons, and started a family, having two sons in two years. As I look back now, I see clearly that my sons were the blessings that God used to open my heart to Jesus Christ.

For the next seven years, I worked as a grunt for a master carpenter, did odd jobs like bush-hogging, fixing broken fences, and bailing hay. And slowly, I became an active part of the community. I attended church with schoolteachers and coal miners and I would stare at the congregation, wondering if I could ever be accepted as a normal member of a community built around peace and harmony. I even got to know the Sheriff and his wife as friends. Imagine that.

One man who made a profound difference in my life was Ray Grimitt. Ray would hire me to do some of the odd jobs on his farm and would always speak of the power of Christ in his life. And when he invited me in for meals, and prayed over food, he would read from a Bible. As several years passed, I was drawn to ask him questions about his religious beliefs. Sometimes we would sit at the table and as he read passages from the Bible, I would ask him how he applied it to his life. Ray, the Ledbetter United Methodist Church, and a pastor by the name of Brother Mike Grimes all were instrumental in planting seeds of curiosity in me. Those seeds would be a major force in winning the battle to win back my soul.

But after seven years of making solid efforts to escape my dark past, and after working and hoping to find peace…the charges from my past came back to haunt me. The federal government issued a warrant for my arrest on racketeering, and the state of Iowa was closing in on me for a murder I had committed. …………I ran.

I hid out in the woods for two weeks. In one sense I was sure I was losing it. I found myself screaming and crying to God, and then, of course, started to question whether He was even real. I had a 44 caliber hand gun with me as well as a long rifle, and I was thinking seriously about simply killing everyone responsible for getting me indicted. After all, no witnesses would equal no sentence for me. But I had left that life, and there was no way I could return to that way of destruction.

I also thought about killing myself in the woods…and as I pressed the barrel of that 44 mag against my head, the old familiar surge of "Do it….Do it Dad….Do it," left me. Forever.

On my tenth day in the woods, I pounded a hole in the ground with my fists, and Christ spoke to me:

"Give your life to me… fully, completely. Serve Me Ron…kill yourself with Me. If you kill others, then the law kills you. If you kill yourself, you're gone. Either way, what do those two answers leave for your sons to follow? Kill yourself with me. You know what it is to have a boss…to obey."

I had worn out my hands, beating that unforgiving ground, and I screamed, "Yes, forgive me, my Boss, for what I've done!" Right there on the spot I surrendered my life to Jesus Christ, and vowed "from this day forward you are my boss…no other."

I told Him "You are now Uno, my boss. Teach me the by-laws of this gang. Lead me to live what I will enforce." Interesting, looking back, that I was applying my old gang-world terminology to my fresh religious vows. And that's one of the things about God that continues to amaze me. He never gave up on this old boy. And, he ain't nervous about any issue, baggage, blood, sh-t, or vomit that dwells in our hearts when we cross over and give our life

to him. Because when it's too dark and cold for everybody else…
it's just right for The Lord. Christ accepted me with all of my pain,
poison, murder, and destruction. I know now that he loves me too
much to leave me the way I came to him.

No, he didn't give up on me. He pressed His pure, clean,
renewing lips against my vomit-filled mouth and sucked the
most screaming pain, fear, and powerlessness *out* of me. Then He
breathed into me the hope that can't be explained in words. Jesus
Christ directed me to choose life over death and it was Jesus Christ
that called me to give myself up. After nearly two weeks in the
woods, I turned myself in to the authorities. My own decision,
my own choice.

The Feds said they would charge me with racketeering, but the
murder charge would be up to the State of Iowa. God and I talked
about the many choices that "we," not I, had to make. The mother
of my children said she would leave me when I went to prison,
despite the fact that I'd been with her for eleven plus years. She
kept her promise and I had to wrap my head around the fact that
my sons Kabe and Garrett, the two life forces who helped me to
see the light, would grow up without me.

I can't begin to place on paper the various talks or arguments,
not to mention screams and cries that I shared with my Father,
God. Even though God was now the leader of my life, I wasn't
agreeing with all the orders He was giving. But I listened, and
learned (and am still learning) to obey. I gave myself up—and
the price would be 58 years in prison. But I gave myself up for
Jesus Christ. Now, I would no longer live for myself…it would be
Christ living within me.

I began my sentence in Greenville FCI Federal Prison, but
was later transferred to one of the most dangerous prisons in the
country, the Maximum Federal Penitentiary in Leavenworth,
Kansas. I won't go into the depths of darkness that breeds in a
maximum prison, but trust me; it's no walk in the park. When my
federal racketeering sentence was fully served, I was transferred
to Iowa to serve the consecutive second-degree murder sentence.

Ghosts from The Past

You talk about fate...the very same guard I had beaten mercilessly back at the Iowa State Pen two decades ago, was now the Deputy Warden at this prison. We had literally torn the hair from his scalp and left him for dead.

I looked across the over-polished gym floor and there he stood, like an apparition. I just stared at him and prayed, 'Lord, what should I do? What can I possibly say that would make any sense?' Then, somehow I found the courage to walk over to him and was given the strength to say, "I am seriously sorry for the pain I have caused you in your life. I now serve Christ Jesus, and I don't want to cause trouble to anyone, except the powers of darkness."

He stood for a frozen moment, looking at me in disbelief. I put out my hand for him to shake. And after what seemed like an eternal pause, he shook my outstretched hand and said, "I've told myself I'd never do this."

I have since come to know that this was a miracle of reconciliation only God could produce. The entire year I was at his prison, the Deputy Warden was supportive of me, and allowed me to come to the I.F.I. (InnerChange Freedom Initiative) Christian program at another prison in Iowa and eventually arranged my transfer there. Later, the Deputy Warden became Warden there as well. God works in strange but deliberate ways.

While in the I.F.I. Christian program at Newton Prison, a civilian walked into the prison to survey the work of the I.F.I. program. His name was Ken Lockard. Two decades earlier, we were mortal enemies. He was a self-appointed tough guy athlete back then, and I had told him that because he had interfered with gang business at the time, I would kill him...as the saying goes, it wasn't a threat, it was a promise. Soon after this promise, I went to prison for my first sentence.

Not knowing we had both since become soldiers in Christ, he recoiled at the sight of me. I picked him out of the crowd, walked over to greet him and shook his hand. It took him a while to believe that an evil bastard like me could've ever become a brother in Christ...a fellow soldier in the Lord's war against hopelessness.

But after he realized that I was for real we cried, prayed, and broke bread together. As a man who has seen darkness that no person should, I now can state, beyond the shadow of any doubt, that Jesus Christ is the light in my life. I can't place on paper the blessings that God graced me with by being allowed to go through the I.F.I. InnerChange program.

As for my dad…with Christ's help I was able to contact him a few years prior to his death. He had made a trip with my aunt to visit me once in prison. It had been 40 years since I had seen that face. We didn't breathe a word about the past; we just made small talk. I thought I'd try to forge some kind of a relationship with him, so that when I got out of prison…just maybe…he could answer those tough questions. But that never happened. I forgave him in the sense that I prayed for his salvation. In doing so, I was able to free a piece of the prisoner…that prisoner being me.

Now

I stay in spiritual warfare, and God remains faithful. In our current prison facility, the Warden allows us to maintain our own church body. The inmates can pick from a full range of belief systems, from Christian to satan worship. I'm honored to have become one of the Christian pastors here every Saturday and Sunday, and I've come to view prison as a village - no different than a village in Africa, Belize, or Brazil. It's true that I surrendered myself willingly to serve my time in prison, but it's also true that I have since surrendered myself to Jesus Christ and will devote my life and every ounce of energy I possess to share the Lord's love with those who think they are alone in this world.

As you know, the law can make a man sit in a cell for years, and if he's done wrong, rightly so. Day after day, month after month, year after year he serves his time, but what's being done to really change him and keep him from returning to prison?

When faith changes a man's heart, he has no choice but to change his behavior. When serving God, a man must believe in something greater than himself. The words and principles of Jesus are in the Bible for us to learn, inspire our imagination, and provide us the means to help others. God has empowered us to be disciples—men who pray. Men who are still learning to strip the baggage of their destructive past...in exchange for the inheritance they have as sons of God versus sons of silence.

My past was deeply entrenched in the world of gangs, both in and out of the penitentiary. I was extremely angry, dark, and violent. But God has a divine mission for each of us, and that includes me.

I now live by standards and values I was once blind to. I see women and those of different race as my equals. I see children as our greatest treasures. I know that lip service does not cut it. So I will allow my actions to speak for whom I serve.

As I write this, I have served over 15 years in prison and I've several more yet to go. I've been mentored by others, and now by the grace of God, it's my turn to mentor and invest in new members of the village we've formed. It is by His grace alone that we are allowed a gift called 'freedom' in Christ. Investing in people is our calling...our mission. We're called to invest in each other as God invests in us, while we exist inside this larger perimeter called earth.

Ultimately, state and federal prisoners will be released back into our community—700,000 of them each year. 67% of those released will be re-arrested and go straight back to a life of incarceration. But for prisoners following an I.F.I. or Prison Fellowship Ministries program, the re-arrest rate is cut by *more than half.* The impact of faith is...undeniable.

I was *given* this opportunity. Yes, given. May God bless you and may you choose to allow Him to navigate your life.

Ron Gruber

MICAH 7:7-9

Ron Gruber can be written directly via Corrlinks.com:
learn more about him and his mailing address at
SonsofGrace.org

The Marine Sniper

Tim Donnelly

Suicide Target

For as long as I can remember, my life has revolved around gaining acceptance. I've never been sure of the reason. Perhaps it was the early diagnosis of Attention Deficit Disorder, or perhaps it was the lack of discipline in my upbringing. But it's hard to put a finger on the real cause.

Despite my enthusiastic and passionate nature as a young child, I always had this insecurity about why I didn't get invited places. The question on my mind was, 'why didn't people want to be friends with me?'

I was sure there had to be something wrong with me, I just didn't know what it was. Longing to fit in, showing off came naturally; I wanted all eyes on me--all the time.

Winning was everything (especially in sports), and I was a terrible loser. I remember getting in trouble for not allowing the neighborhood kids win at anything. For me, winning was acceptance. Losing was rejection.

I was 12 years old when, like a lot of others, I took my first drink stolen from my father's liquor cabinet. I remember feeling a warm, sweet rush as it went down, and man, it felt so good! Of the two friends with me on this experiment in chasing "manhood," I was the only one who enjoyed it. But it was more than enjoyment for me. The alcohol warmed my body, dulled my mind, and somehow freed me. For the first time in my life, I didn't care what anyone thought about me. For a young man struggling with acceptance, I thought this new and easy escape would be the answer to my problems.

By the time I hit high school, drugs and alcohol overtook my insane desire to win. I was still playing sports, but now there was something better to take away the pain of my insecurities. Escaping from who I was became my only mission.

High school ended, and sports gave me the ticket to a well-known university playing lacrosse. On the surface, you'd think everything was fine. I was a Division 1 player at one of the top universities in the country. To my friends, I was just another freshman jock doing some occasional recreational drugs. The real picture was much darker.

But it was too late to reorder my life. My life, if you could call it that, was ruled by addictions. Having come from a family of alcoholics, I knew where I was headed. Having grown up around my hard-drinking grandfather and uncle, I saw the mortal and debilitating stigmas. I felt as if my life was going to be worthless, and there was little doubt I would end up just like them. Racing toward certain destruction, in my own scrambled mind, I was sure the world would be a better place without me.

It was then that I decided to end my life...

In one afternoon I took over 375 pills: 150 Ritalin, 150 Prozac, and 75 Tylox, chasing them down with none other than Southern Comfort. And as I swallowed, I wrote the following suicide note:

Suicide

Paranoid delusions. Twisted thoughts of love and hate.

Hate for life and love for death.

Hell awaits me as my eternal resting place.

Wishing to hurt no one, just putting an end to my own pain.

Pain in the failure of a wasted life.

Pills, drugs, guns, and smoke are the pictures that will tell the story of my conclusion.

I have loved those who loved me.

I run. Run from life, run from society, run from the pain buried amidst the waves of my thoughts.

I'm sorry for the pain I cast.

Selfish maybe, but this intense need for death overwhelms me.

I fantasize about the feel of the cold barrel in my mouth or the feel of the trigger on my finger.

I tremble with fear of what is to come, but that fear is overcome by a desire for death.

I wish to run.

Running will help me not, for you cannot run from whom you are.

Nor can one run from the feelings he hides.

I ask for God's pity. The Sin of all Sins. Hell is my sentence.

There is no one, No one who can help me, for I am beyond help.

I love everyone but my insecurity prevails.

Prevailing over the feeling of love and acceptance that I long to feel.

Why me God? Why this Life?

Life or Death. I choose Death. Help is nowhere to be found. HELP ME PLEASE.

As I feel the drugs beginning to kick in, I feel that my end is near.

I bring it upon myself, therefore no one must bear responsibility for the sin I commit.

I love all of you.

All apologies to those whom I hurt with this fate that is at hand.

It is time to end this meaningless life.

It is time to end this life of inferiority. This life I can no longer live.

A rest in Hell I do not know. The only knowledge is that I am unsuitable for this life.

Unsuitable for society. Unable to serve those who care so much.

I wish to live but realize that death is my only answer. How weak I am.

He who cannot bear the pain of emotions and the struggle of life must take fate into his own hands; hence he must seal his fate and take the life he no longer chooses to live! Happiness evades this child of God, which will make his life unbearable to live, and of no value to society.

Let all rejoice for my pain is gone.

• • •

Perhaps mentioning God in my note was a sign that I still had enough will to live, making one last phone call for help. When my sister arrived, she found me unconscious and dying. She brought me back to consciousness just long enough for the ambulance to arrive and save my pitiful life. I could barely see the doctors and nurses through my self-induced haze, while they were busy pumping my stomach. My father was next to the bed, crying as he said over and over, "Everything's going to be okay."

Later in ICU, my father was right by my side. His serious tone brought me up short when he said, "What you did to yourself...you should be dead, but God has a purpose for you and he's not ready to let you go just yet. I don't know what his plan for you is...but, I'll tell you this; you need to figure it out quickly because, right now, by all rights, you should be dead!"

You'd think that I would've gotten the message loud and clear. You'd think, after all that, I'd have nowhere to go but up. Yes, I was admitted to a treatment facility for 30 days. But like many others who have been through the struggle, I was just going through the motions. I would smile while deceiving everyone, especially those who were trying to help me and...even succeeding at fooling myself at times. And then, right on cue, I went back to drugs and alcohol.

I decided to make another move, clear cross-country to Missoula, Montana where no one I knew would be on hand to watch me dive back into the bottle. I proceeded to hook up with a woman eight years older, and just as dysfunctional. Our relationship was based entirely on alcohol abuse. And of course we made the addict's time-honored mistake of thinking our mutual need was the same as true love, and tied the knot. But, as usual, it wasn't long before I was ready to run again. I left her and the marriage flat in the middle of the night, to join the Marines.

Looking For a Few Good Men

The Marine Corps was a gift and did it's best to heal me. I'll always be grateful. It built a level of confidence in me that I never had the faintest chance of realizing. I fit the model of a "true renegade." "Live fast and die young" was the rule that governed my life and my action; picture-perfect malleable material for the Corps. But my old habits were far too large and in charge. No more than six months after joining, I wanted out. I was ready to run again.

I began researching some kind of workable exit strategy and came across the Marine Corps substance abuse program, called Level III Treatment. After a little more digging I was sure this would be my ticket home. The regulations stipulated that if a soldier got recommended for treatment and then declined it, he would be discharged..... Perfect!

So, moving forward with my plan, I proceeded to down a fifth of rum on a daily basis. And after 28 days of solid drinking I, of course, began to think about ending my life again. But this time the vicious cycle was premeditated.

I phoned my brother to let him in on the plan and "for the record" told him that I was having suicidal thoughts. He, in turn, immediately called the base officer of the day who, going by the book, turned me in. All according to plan, I was recommended for treatment ASAP. ......Great! I thought I had just beaten the system. The only problem was that the regulations pertaining to treatment and dismissal had changed to read, 'any Marine refusing psychological treatment would be dishonorably discharged.' With that on my permanent record, I wouldn't even be able get a job at McDonalds—it is the most reprehensible badge of shame in the military —one that I surely didn't want to wear for the duration of my life.

Turning the Corner

So, without the slightest bit of good intention, I entered the Marine Corps treatment program and was forced to stay sober for one year. The completion of that brutal year of sobriety seemed to mark a new beginning for me. I finally set a clear-headed goal, deciding to become a Marine Scout Sniper. I trained for that position with more intensity and determination than anything I'd ever attempted. After nine months of training, I absolutely aced my indoctrination, finishing in the top 5 of the 52 men who tried out. As a newly minted Scout Sniper, I had become truly one of the few, one of the proud—in one of the most elite units in the United States Marine Corps.

Highly trained and deadly efficient in the craft of my choosing, I was a natural choice when the Corps was looking for someone to instruct the next generation of Snipers. But my term in the Marines was done, and declined to re-up. Freshly mustered out of the Marines, I didn't last 24 hours before I bought a bag of weed and got high. I thought I'd turned a major corner in my life, but all I had done was take a sharp u-turn, heading straight back to my same old MO. Without the Corps, I had no structure in my life and there wasn't a day that went by that I didn't get stoned on anything available. You'd think I would have taken the acceptance I had found through sobriety and put it to good use, but I was too far-gone.

I moved back home and drank everyday. I continued to do so for two years solid. My mom could barely stand the sight of me and was sick of my lame excuses. So I ran again. This time I escaped to the sun-drenched lifestyle of southern California.

Another definite wrong turn. Unfortunately for me, California has always been an addict's heaven. All the wrong things were just too accessible. And it wasn't long before my alcohol and drug use became too radical, even for the people I was hanging with. Imagine that; I was too messed up for California. It became obvious to me, even in my delusional condition, that I'd have to leave or die. So it was back to Montana to be near my brother. I was grasping for anything solid to hold on to.

For the first time in my life, I was given the rare opportunity to live off the beaten path in Frenchtown, Montana, completely isolated from the mad rush of civilization. I picked up some day work doing manual labor, and aside from my time spent on the job, drinking and doing drugs occupied every waking moment, despite my peaceful surroundings.

One day, I was driving home drunk. The road was slick with black ice, very common to Montana in the winter. I lost control and rolled my Explorer twice. The frame was crushed. The roof caved in to a position only eight inches from my head. I wasn't even wearing a seat belt and I walked away from that wreck completely unscathed, not even a scratch on me. God had most definitely touched my life. And still I was saying "Not now" to God. I pushed him away just as casually as I had dusted the snow off my jacket, strolling mindlessly away from disaster.

Two months later my sister-in-law called me at work and told me that my dog Sadie had bitten the neighborhood mailman and my only true friend would have to be put down. But being the ex-Marine, hard case that I was; I was determined to put the dog down by shooting her myself.

Especially in times of crisis, liquor was my security blanket of choice. I was on the way home to shoot Sadie, and pulled into the first bar on the road home. One drink naturally led to the next and I was pretty wasted when I headed back out to my car. A mile down the snow-filled road, I lost control again and drove into a ditch. Minutes later, the cops were on the scene, threw me in jail, and slapped me with my first DUI. The near misses were accumulating and there was bound to be a day of reckoning.

It happened that same night. My sister-in-law had come to my rescue and bailed me out of jail. While she was driving me home, it hit me. I realized what anyone watching from the cheap seats would have seen years earlier; whenever I drank, bad things happened. I stopped drinking, cold turkey, that night and gradually, over time, began to become more aware of who I was. Saying no to that monkey on my back was undoubtedly the hardest thing I'd ever had to do, but things started to change for the better and I was slowly becoming comfortable living in my own skin.

And Another U-Turn

I was able to lower the curtain on the sideshow I had been putting on for all those years, and finally be me. One sunlit Saturday afternoon I met a girl, who today is my beautiful wife. We started out fine but three months after we first met, while we were on vacation, I had "just one" drink to feel at ease with my friends.

I lept back on the drinking train with a vengeance, and that train started to gather speed at an alarming rate. Even the woman of my dreams took a back seat to Mr. Jack Daniels.

With each passing day, my addiction grew stronger.

Early one morning I got a call. My father had had a stroke the night before and was in the hospital. Something in my heart told me that he wasn't going to make it. Just two days earlier, we had talked about me going to work for him. Father & Son, Inc. It would involve me moving back home. He had been so excited. This was the man who had always believed in me and had never stopped believing. Yet even as we hatched our business plan, I wasn't sure if I could ever overcome my demons. He was sure. He believed in me more than I ever could. And with this bad news, my new dream-come-true was crumbling before my eyes.

Time stood still as I waited to leave from the Montana airport. By the time I arrived at the hospital, the swelling on his brain was so bad that he no longer had the power to speak. He slowly reached out and barely grasped my thumb with his hand. The tears were welling up as I said, "Dad, I'm sorry I've let you down." Throughout my entire life, my father was the one man who believed the world was mine. From my future as an athlete to my career plans, he always believed I would arrive at the top. He was so proud of me, and loved me more than I ever loved myself.

As I saw it, all I'd ever done was disappoint this man. And now, the only thing I wanted was to be reassured by him, but he couldn't even speak. If I could've asked God for anything that moment it would have been for his last words to me be, "I Love you Son and you never let me down."

The decision was made to take him off life support. And for some reason, I remember feeling compelled to wash his feet before he died. I was desperate to do something for him, and also gain his forgiveness. I had remembered the story of Jesus washing the feet of the disciples. So I grabbed a hospital hand towel and started to wash his feet while apologizing for everything I'd ever done to him and everything I'd ever thought I'd done wrong in my life. I look back and wonder why I washed his feet and I attribute it to one of the greatest lessons anyone can ever learn; one my father had gone out of his way to teach me. The lesson of forgiving other people their sins. In my case, I'd have to learn how to forgive myself.

Throughout my roller coaster life, my mom and dad had always continued to love and support my every dream. No matter how much I messed up or how many times my behavior hurt them, they always forgave me. They had exposed my siblings and I, as kids, to a selection of churches, pointing us gently toward finding religion in our own time and in our own way. At the moment my father lay there dying, I somehow felt sure that God existed and that he would forgive, love, and protect me. Now it was up to me to share in his forgiveness.You would think that my father's passing would've been a huge motivator to get serious about finding myself and freeing myself from my alcohol and prescription crutches, but it seemed that I was resolved to continue my "Not now" stance concerning God. And, of course, without God by my side my life continued to spiral down once again.

The level of grief I was experiencing was even deeper than it had been before my original suicide attempt. Barely conscious for the next 18 months, I became completely useless. I was slumped on the couch one miserable afternoon and slurred to myself, "I'm a waste and would be better off dead."

But this time, it was God who stepped in and told me 'Not now.' "You will not kill yourself. Not Now."

I got up off the couch and I went over to my mom's. I told her how I was feeling. All she said was, "You know what you gotta do."

The next day I got up and went to work. That night, I went to a meeting. I heard everything I needed to hear that very first night. I realize that throughout my life, I've always had the heart for God...a vague yearning to walk down the right path, but no directions to find it. What I learned at that AA meeting gave me the key to unlock the secret for my survival. The key that would save my life was finally realizing that I needed to surrender my life to God.

I went home that night, and I got on my knees and said, "I

can't do this anymore, Lord. I'm turning my life over to your care because under my control my life is a mess."

And with that I turned my will and my life over to the care of God. It was at that moment that I stopped saying "not now" and began saying. "OK Lord...now." Now I'm ready.

Now

That was the beginning of God's time. I went back to all the books I had collected and began reading everything I could get my hands on concerning self-discovery and worked diligently at following the program God had planned for my life. I surrounded myself with other people whose problems and goals were similar to mine; and every day I moved one inch closer, towards the life that I had always wanted.

I still struggled with acceptance and I still wanted everyone to like me. Nothing changed yet, with the exception of the strength I always found in God. Time passed and I was building a solid foundation for a new way of life, a foundation built on prayer. I would begin each day on my hands and knees asking God to take control of my life for just one more day, and at night I would thank him for all that he'd done for me. Every day I surrendered my life to what God wanted for me, and not what I wanted for myself.

I was doing God's will and the life I was living began to improve exponentially.

But even though I had conquered the addictions which ruled me for so long, other demons began to surface. The devil knew I was weak and was relentless in his pursuit of my soul. Greed, lust, and envy raised their ugly heads and began to show themselves in every aspect of my life. The very same spiritual battle that everyone hears about, between God and the Devil, was being fought – my soul as the prize for the winner. The dark power fighting the Lord was working every trick in his thick book. He was intent on getting me to say, "Not now" to the Lord just one more time.

Shortly after getting sober, I began attending a Men's Gospel Reflection Group, mostly former 'tough guys,' now on God's journey to finding out who they were, where they were, and hopefully where they were going. It was there that I began to realize the importance of my faith. I began believing in something greater than myself, finally understanding the intrinsic truth that I am nobody without God.

Working among this group of men has made a very real difference in my life. Early on, one man took me out to lunch and resparked the confidence that has grown steadily within me ever since. He turned me on to five books that changed his life and, in his opinion, would be instrumental in changing any man's life. They were:

How to Win Friends and Influence People by Dale Carnegie
The Power of Your Sub-conscious Mind by Norman Vincent Peale
The Greatest Salesman in The World by Og Mandino
Tough Times Never Last but Tough People Do by Robert Schueller
And last, but certainly not the least, The Holy Bible

God began to show me new things about my life—but not particularly flattering things. I saw how much I envied material things that others had. I saw how much I longed for money. But the seeds of Humility, Judgment, Honesty, and Justice had been planted, and they were all more than ready to be harvested.

Am I perfect now? Far from it. But the more and more I continue to say 'now' to God, the more I am blessed. I am not the same man I once was. As Saul said to Paul in Galatians 2:19, 20, "It is no longer me who lives…but Christ who lives in me." I now know that God allowed me to see the error of my ways, protected me from suicide, and averted many failures.

Today my life is far from easy. Every day spent on the spiritual path brings a host of challenges. The Lord can change your life if you let him, but the hardest part is that first step of surrender. As in any learning process, it's always the first step which is the hardest.

I'll leave you with this: I hope and pray that my words, or the words of any of the other nine men who've been brave enough to tell their stories in this book, inspire you to take that first step. Because I promise you that once you are able to entrust your darkest fears to a higher power, you will know the true meaning of freedom.

Just know this:

Jesus loves you.

God loves you. And he will never forsake you.

Tim Donnelly

▨▨▨

The Contractor

Bobby Ciampitti

Mafia Associate vs. Street Apostle

"I am not proud of everything I've done in life, but I regret nothing. I did what had to be done to prevent others from doing to me what I was about to do to them. People may not like or respect me but they will fear me. We are all players on this game board called life and the fact that I have achieved a better understanding of how the game works and how to win, does not make me an evil person. I simply possess the ability to foresee a Check coming and always am able to retaliate with nothing less than a Check Mate."

There comes a time in everyone's life when we must face the actuality of our existence; a time when we must put aside rationalization or the veil of false justification to weigh the entirety of our lives against the one-dimensional list of our personal accomplishments. This has to be done with cold, objective, and sometimes callous examination. We reach an impasse and every ingredient in the bubbling cauldron of our lives has to be dissected and judged, to be: kept, reworked, reshaped, or completely discarded in order to move forward.

I'm 61 now and I've reached that crossroads three separate times in my life. Each time I've come to a decidedly different conclusion about where I've been and where I am going.

I'm not sure where this writing will lead, or how much I will have the stomach or desire to unearth, but I'll make this promise: I'll be as candid as possible as I reveal secrets I've kept from my own wife and family for more than three decades.

For years I've kept a journal of my life's events: positive and negative, good and evil, successes and failures – everything. And, as I reread those handwritten memories, I have the longing hope that I can learn from them. And, if it's possible, I'd like to correct the wrongs I've done to others and repair the damage I've done to myself.

I have struggled to live with myself by attempting to manipulate my memories. My success in blocking out reality has been intermittent at best. All I've had to work with is my primal will to survive. When I talk about my life, I'm not talking about a life of PTA meetings, bowling, and lawn mowing. I'm talking about a life immersed for decades in the dark world of organized crime. But that was then and this is now, and I'm getting ahead of myself.

Why would I choose to reveal, in the telling of my story, the tactics I used and still have occasion to use - tactics and strategies on how to weigh, measure and dispose of anyone who has ever entered my fighting arena of power, influence and material gain? My timing for revealing these methods of operation is even more questionable, knowing that some of my opponents/enemies are still playing the high-stakes game of life and death with no end in sight. I should just take a deep breath and begin.

Searching for Faith

I was the middle child of a second generation, average Italian-American family. My father worked his way through the depression, and my grandfather ran a small candy store in South Philly. My dad, after returning from World War II, attended night school on the GI Plan and worked during the day toward his eventual career as a real estate broker. It seemed to me, as a young boy, that his evenings were always taken, showing houses or attending classes. I don't recall much interaction with him at all, but I do remember him being there for important things like holidays, family gatherings, evening meals, and any illness which kept me home from school.

My mother was one of seven children, also from a working-class, close-knit Italian family. I had numerous Compares and

Comares, (godfathers and godmothers) and it was growing up around them that gave me invaluable street knowledge, understanding of the law of the jungle - how to get along with others, survive, and prosper.

But I was a restless kid, and felt that no one took me seriously. I couldn't wait to grow up and show the world what I was capable of; because for me, life was too damn slow. While other kids were out playing with friends and taking life as it came, I was plotting ways to make a few bucks in hopes that I could gain respect and freedom.

At the age of seven, I came up with my first enterprise: running errands for neighbors who were at home raising children and maintaining a household. This was a start but it lacked any "growth potential" since my parents enforced a three-city-block limit for me to do business. Next, it was painting street addresses on the curbs for homeowners, painting iron railings and yard fences, followed by charging for the return of empty trash cans to neighbors after weekly trash pickups. Of course, like every east-coast kid, I would shovel snow and clear snow off cars to add to my already impressive income.

In order to protect my income from the other neighborhood kids trying to encroach on my territory or cash in on my ideas, I made a habit out of collecting a small deposit from my clients to make sure they didn't jump ship and decide to hook up with the competition mid-contract. Although all this seems fairly sophisticated for a seven-year old kid, it was just 'taking care of business' for me. Now that I had contracts, I needed help. I recruited my neighborhood friends to work for a fair wage, which kept competition to a minimum. If someone gave work to another kid instead of me, I would have one of the local bullies track them down and convince them to stay out of my turf. Of course this tactic also required a small fee, which I was happy to pay.

When I was eight, a new Catholic Parish opened in the neighborhood with its own elementary school. My best friend Alfred was enrolled to start third grade in the fall and I was determined to join him. After telling my parents how important it was to me, they agreed to enroll my older brother, Bill and me.

September came and I was one of sixty-two children sitting in a brand new classroom waiting and wishing for my world to change. I got my wish. My first day was filled with firsts. It was the first time I had ever seen a nun up close and the first time I ever spoke to a priest one-on-one. I was surrounded by the image of Jesus Christ, who up to that point I had only read about. This was it, I thought. I found a way for adults to take me seriously and maybe listen to what I had to say, and how I felt about a variety of topics. Yes, eight years old and I wanted to be just like Christ... with all my heart, I wanted to be a priest!

Faith – the First Exposure

I collected my friends and a posse of workers, and outlined the new idea for combining my ambition with more steady income. We had a list of steady clients, all of whom had children of varying ages who we could recruit for the new...drum roll... "Children's Church." Every one of my friends and workers followed my lead. We went around collecting items needed to set up a church in my basement. I put on my black Sunday suit, black shirt, and white collar along with black felt hat. I had rosary beads on my belt, and with Sunday Missal in hand and my team of eight-year old apostles, we went door to door talking about Jesus Christ. I asked the homeowners if I could bless their house with a bottle of holy water that I "borrowed" from the fountain at school, and then politely asked for a small donation, giving some of it to Catholic Charities Appeal and the "Pagan Babies Fund" (a legitimate charity for orphaned children).

After weeks of observing every detail of the mass held at church, I began holding my version of mass in my parent's basement every Saturday at 6:00 pm. I used grape juice for wine and white NECO Wafers for Communion. And of course I passed a wicker basket for offerings. Even some of the adult neighbors came to watch as their children equaled or bettered what they witnessed at church every Sunday.

No one was laughing at me now, they were amazed. My peers were looking up to me, following my lead, and even obeying my orders. Kids were lined up to join our group. At the age of eight, I already possessed the uncanny ability to motivate people to do things they would normally never do. However, my parents were concerned. Many years later, my father told me he feared my ability to influence others without regard as to how to handle such a responsibility. He knew that unchained power like that, came with consequences. He also knew that my newfound abilities were not normal for a boy of my age. He was afraid that I would follow my own will with no ability to apply the brakes. He hoped that by controlling my activities he could keep me from the harm that would inevitably come. I was already beyond warning, and just as he feared, became consumed with my unusual talent.

"Rather than follow in the footsteps of those who have gone before you, cut a new path and leave a trail."

I thought I was on the right path. I had embraced the quote above as my new code. But something else was going on inside my head. I didn't exactly know what it was, but there was a force at work, unseen, quiet yet purposeful, driving me in an unknown direction. Good is easy to recognize, but I know now that Evil can appear in many forms. How could an eight year-old be expected to see beyond a dream come true.

Faith Lost

At nine, I was feeling the weight of responsibility. My friends and team of workers were depending on *me* for every new move. They were excited at their ability to do and accomplish things that no other kids were doing at that time. We had a following of kids, both younger and older, but the fun had turned into work.

I sat in class the first day of fourth grade, waiting to see who my teacher would be that year. I found myself thinking of how I could use what I had learned to help other kids. I knew that I was lucky; I had loving parents and a large immediate family of grandparents, aunts, uncles, cousins and caring neighbors.

Then it happened. My daydreaming about happiness and

the good we were creating in the world at such a young age, was shattered. My life was about to take a sharp turn because of one person.

The classroom door opened, slammed against the wall, and there stood a tall, skinny St. Joseph's nun with a stern jaw and sour smile. She was motionless and speechless, arms neatly concealed in the sleeves of her habit, a heavy wooden ruler protruding from one of the sleeves. I would soon discover that the ruler was not for measuring but for cracking the knuckles of any child not in compliance with the rules of this enforcer.

There she stood taking mental inventory of about sixty students sitting before her, hands and arms folded, shaking in their seats, waiting for venom to spew from her lifeless white lips.

It seemed like an eternity before she spoke. Then she wrote her God forsaken name, Sister Emunda Marie, on the blackboard with a large piece of white chalk that screeched as if it were an omen of bad things to come... and the omen was accurate.

She was the worst kind of Catholic that existed in the mind of a nine year-old Italian boy. A pale-white Irish Catholic Nun with an open dislike for Italians. She was prejudice incarnate. God must have a sense of humor I thought, why else would he send her to a 98% Italian parish? Perhaps God didn't much care for her either. She was what my mother referred to later as a frustrated virgin. My mother was usually right when it came to people, especially concerning their treatment of children.

It didn't take long before she isolated several boys in the class to torture on a regular basis, while the Irish girls found favor in her totalitarian world. By mid-October, she had isolated and weeded out two thankless souls from her flock, me and my friend Anthony.

Each day began with a barrage of derogatory comments. She would regularly lock us in the coat closet; and open the closet door occasionally to douse us with Holy Water, claiming we were possessed by the devil. Tears now form in my eyes as I recall those dark days of being locked in that closet day after day. But, in retrospect, I should actually write that bitch a thank you note for making me stronger than ever, and more determined than ever.

I was thrown a lifeline that year, but perhaps it was thrown too late. For no special reason, I was auditioning for the choir and was told I had the perfect range to sing high soprano. I had no idea what that meant, but it seemed that I was the only one who could reach those notes.

My newly discovered talent made me a hot commodity for the parish and the pastor made sure I got plenty of hours of practice. This required me to be absent from Sister Witch's classroom on a regular basis. I took full advantage of my escape hatch, but poor Anthony was not so lucky. I thought of him every day the rest of that year.

Because of that nun, I shut down the Children's Church. Those in authority of the real parish had no idea what the Bible taught, and if God could allow children to be locked in closets and be put in the same category as the devil, then from here on out God was on his own. At age nine, the church was dead to me. I could take care of myself....or, at least I thought I could.

The Hook is Baited

I began to expand my horizons by becoming a shoe-shine boy at the pool hall at the end of my street. No one under twenty-one was allowed in, but newspaper boys and shoe-shine boys were exempt. As I soon found out, this wasn't any normal pool hall... not by any stretch of the imagination.

Although my mother saw no harm in my little business, she warned me that my father would not approve. And she agreed to keep our little secret, as long as I was home in time for dinner.

The pool hall had a clientele of many diverse and interesting men. You might call them "Wise Guys." In fact, that's exactly what they were. One day while earning ten cents for a shine, I was asked if I knew where the Porter House Tap Room was.

I said, "Yes, just a few blocks up the street."

"That's right," he said. "How would you like to do a few shines for some friends of mine who run the joint?" He told me he would make it worth my while and handed me a dollar bill and a dime for the shine.

I smiled as I answered, "Sure!" It was within my allowable geographic limits and a dollar was a lot of money for a nine year-old.

"Great," he said. "Just ask for Jim and while you're doing his shine, slip him this little piece of paper. He'll give you another dollar and a dime for the effort."

Wow!! Two dollars and twenty cents for one hour's worth of work.

When I got to the Porter House and met Jim, the scenario was exactly as it was described, with one exception.

Jim asked me if I knew where the hardware store was on the corner of Shunk and Mildred Street. Of course I knew; my house was only one block away.

"Well," he added, "if you wouldn't mind stopping there on your way home it would be worth the trip." He assured me his friend Harry would love a shine would make it worth my while.

And so I followed his instructions to the letter and true to his word "Harry the Horse" was there, waiting for a shine and the little pieces of paper Jim had given me at the Tap Room.

Things were starting to look up. Three times a week I would perform this delivery ritual and earn three dollars and thirty cents for the effort. This was all on top of the money I made from other patrons at the pool hall and the Tap Room.

Averaging twenty-five dollars a week from the shoe-shine business, plus fifteen dollars from my various other ventures, netted me $40 in a good week. To put this in perspective, the year was 1957 and the average working man netted $60-$70 a week for a full forty hours of labor. I was nine and was bringing home 2/3 of what the man on the street was earning.

I became a staple at those establishments and very friendly with some of the "Wise Guys" who looked out for me. By the time I was ten, I was loaning money to guys playing pool and the "Wise Guys" showed me how to maximize this by collecting twice the amount loaned by week's end. In the event someone didn't pay up, the boys would persuasively ensure my 'clients' would come up with the money to pay me.

So by age ten, I was running numbers and running a mini loan shark operation. I had no idea that this had anything to do with going down "the wrong road." Experience had taught me that this was just how the world worked, and I sure didn't mind the money.

By the time I reached eighth grade, we had moved from our small neighborhood to a large house on Broad Street, complete with new furniture and a new car in the driveway. My dad had always taught us to live below our means and always be humble and caring for others. If this was below our means, I thought, then we must be doing pretty well, but I still hadn't learned to appreciate my dad and his ways.

I didn't have a great relationship with my dad during that part of my life. He was a kind, soft-spoken man who always found compromise to be a better solution than confrontation. I didn't agree and thought him to be somewhat of a pushover. I had grossly misjudged him, and misunderstood his acts of kindness for weakness...and that would come back to bite me in the ass later in life.

While my Dad worked and attended school at night, I had another male role model, my Uncle Nick. He lived across the street and I saw him at least twice a day.

He was a mountain of a man with a strong sense of confidence and self-respect. He walked with a swagger that sent a loud and clear signal, "Don't piss me off." He took crap from nobody, always stood his ground, yet was a friend to everyone in the neighborhood, and someone you could count on when in need or in trouble.

He was a master mechanic with working knowledge of every trade you could imagine and the proper tools to go along with that knowledge. He was someone I could look up to and emulate. His personality was the antithesis of my Dad's.

We had a simple working arrangement. He would take me on side jobs as a helper and as I became proficient at a particular task, he would give me a tool of my own. He had me build a workbench, keeping my tools sharp, clean and organized. I was to use my new skills to make whatever repairs around the house I could and return everything to its proper place. He would come by on a regular basis to make sure I was taking care of my tools. If not, he would take them away until I learned to appreciate their value.

He told me that once I learned a trade, nobody could take that away. It was my Uncle Nick who got me started learning "the trades," which eventually led me to the construction and contracting businesses.

Although I was maturing in many areas, I wasn't feeling any real satisfaction in my accomplishments. A sense of frustration continually hung over me like a dark cloud. I felt I was missing out on something or leaving something on the table that others would take. My parents were concerned about my teenage arrogance and overwhelming determination to succeed at anything, at any cost. They decided to enroll me in a Quaker High School where I would begin ninth grade.

I was not looking forward to trading my tough South Philly gang for a bunch of jacket and tie Quaker geeks. To me, there was something decidedly bizarre about the place. Maybe it was their liberal and permissive policies and style of teaching that was such a shock to my system. I also knew that the opportunities for running any of my profitable street games were going to be few to none. But if having their son safe in a "private school" was going to make my parents happy; then I figured I owed them that. I sucked it up and hoped for the best.

The school was littered with kids from well-to-do families, all spoiled and catered to most of their lives. They had no idea how to survive outside their sheltered existence and had no street smarts whatsoever. They were self-absorbed with moral convictions based on nothing but the ability to buy their way out of uncomfortable situations. Repeat: buy their way out of uncomfortable situations.

To quote a line from the movie My Blue Heaven, *"Where others might see a problem, I see opportunity."*

Now my challenge was to create a problem in this silverspoon crowd, for which I could be the only answer to. It didn't take long for me to get into a fight. I had been listening to the non-stop comments made about me in the hallways, in class, and in the cafeteria. I was one of the only Roman Catholics in the freshman class, and definitely the only Italian. Instead of making an effort to blend in, I decided to stand out with my "mean streets" image, complete with Pompadour hair style, shaved-off side burns, velvet jacket with no collar, iridescent shirt with spaghetti neck tie, and the infamous Matador "fence-climber" boots. I was even carrying a well-constructed Italian switchblade "just in case." I was a walking grenade, just waiting for someone to pull the pin. And someone did. During meditation in the Quaker Meeting Hall, one kid told another, within earshot, "That's the Dago from South Philly in front of us; he thinks he's a hard ass."

Before he knew what hit him, I was making this rich kid's face into ground chuck. My punches had the unrelenting repetition of an automatic weapon as I struck my target over and over. Bingo, I became the problem that people would pay to solve. Sure...I served my obligatory detention time, which the Quaker's called Inner Reflection.

And for the entire time I chose to reflect on how could I make a buck out of this situation.

My answer was selling protection. In a school packed with non-violent peace activists, the school population would need protection from *me*!

I had hundreds of leaflets printed up, all with the image of an ominous black hand and the phrase reading, "Five bucks a week and fear no one!" I slipped it in lockers and folders all over the school, and it wasn't long before I was collecting nearly $300 a month in protection money at age fourteen. And then, to add another point of sale to my services, I offered to find a way into the assistant dean's office and change grades for a fee.

Naturally, I was in the head master's office on a regular basis for one disciplinary action or another, but every time he met with my parents he told them how well I was doing and how much I was liked by the faculty. Of course, this was complete bullsh-t, created to keep the fat tuition checks rolling in. I told my parents if they didn't get me out of there, something bad was going to happen.

By late October of my sophomore year, I had made my escape, with my parents blessing, and was attending Bishop Neumann

High, where I should have gone in the first place. I was back in Catholic School but certainly nowhere near being back in the faith.

Faith Regained - One Man's Influence

Father La Luzerne was a St. Norbert Priest. He played a big role in my life and was someone I came to admire. My family was very fond of this gentle man and he was present at many dinners and functions. He and I became close friends and I would visit him at his rectory to discuss life, my fears, the tormenting abuse from the nun, and my corresponding anger with the church. We also spent many evenings talking about my lost faith. As my confidence in Father La Luzerne grew I was able to gradually let go of my hate and again wanted to strive to be a better person.

During my last few years of high school, this close one-on-one relationship reopened my spiritual side and my relationship with God. I felt complete, and in control of my future. This calmness lasted through my college years and although I fell many times along the way, I was never discouraged. I kept a healthy perspective on my human weaknesses and accepted mine as they were. I knew the forgiveness of my faith and I used it many times to regain the light.

I was on my journey back, but took it slowly. I still had deep wounds from the immeasurable hurt inflicted on me by the masochistic nun. I was still skeptical.

I met my wife, the love of my life, my junior year of high school and my focus shifted to her and our future. From the beginning we knew we were meant for each other and felt very comfortable planning our life together.

When we were married, we were confident that God was pleased with our efforts and was blessing our every decision. Father La Luzerne was still a big part of our young lives, there for us like a beacon, whenever I was in danger of running aground.

Starting a family is an awesome responsibility and I immediately transferred all of my hopes, dreams, and energy to making that happen in the best way possible. More than ever, I became focused on succeeding and the desire to provide everything that my family would ever need.

I wasn't dissatisfied with my faith, family, or fledging career in construction, but I was looking for something to lift my status and circle of influence not usually attained by a 21 year old. I was a strong believer in the adage, "Opportunities are never lost…just taken advantage of by someone else." I kept my eyes and ears open, and my mouth shut. Let everyone underestimate me I thought, that way they'll never see the hammer coming.

Everyday was becoming a push, and success wasn't coming easy. I spent many hours working hard, playing by the rules, and trying to gain a *legitimate* edge. But my business competitors used underhanded and unethical tactics to beat me out of a construction job, or find a way not to pay me.

I became bitter and jaded at how I was being cheated on the front end and then on the back end, of every deal. I'll never forget the day I pounded my fist on a bar and proclaimed, "No more. From here on out I will do *whatever* is necessary to ensure success!" That one word, 'whatever,' would become an equal mixture of good and evil - a high road of ambition leading directly to the lowest road of desperation and desperate deeds.

The High Road

At 24, a call from my friend Pete started me on a path I've been attempting to follow every day since.

"Bob," he said, "what do you know about the Freemasons?"

"Not much," I said. "I spent some time my senior year at Temple University writing a report on the Grand Lodge of Pennsylvania Masonic Temple at One North Broad Street from an architectural point of view, and picked up some knowledge on the fraternity. But nothing deep, why?"

"A friend of mine, Harry, asked if I would be interested in learning more about it and maybe applying for membership?" So Pete asked, "Would you be interested too?"

After a short pause, I said, "Yes."

I did some research on the ancient fraternal order and was

amazed at what I found. They were a group of men aspiring to reach a higher standard of character with commitment to do whatever they could to improve and raise the level of social behavior for the betterment of all mankind. Wow... and their success record was excellent.

Everyone from George Washington and Benjamin Franklin to Stephen Gerard and Harry Truman were Freemasons, and I anxiously wanted to become a member too. And when the invitation came, I was excited beyond belief.

I was 24, and was being welcomed into the oldest, most respected and influential organization in the history of the world. What mysteries would I be able to uncover? What would I learn about life that I had not yet experienced? I had been in the Temple building many times before but always wondered what went on when the "Masons" were in the Lodge.

The more I attended, the more I craved knowledge about its mysteries and teachings. All the rumors I'd ever heard about the Masons turned out to be false. What I discovered, was how closely their teachings were to my Christian faith. The Masons, although not a religious organization, won't accept an application from anyone not believing in a supreme being. Their feeling is that if you don't believe in an eventual day of judgement by your maker; you'll have no reason to fear retributions for actions or how you treat others in this life. That is the lone religious premise of the Masonic Organization and they take it seriously. But at the time, the Catholic Church frowned on parishioners becoming members and I was amazed to learn that a Catholic could've been excommunicated for joining.

Nevertheless, it was the Freemasons, after I joined, who gave me my first big break in my business life, awarding me a lucrative contract lasting more than three years, and stabilizing my fledgling company. When confronted by a visiting priest from our parish about my association with the fraternity, I told him I couldn't recall a similar contract coming from the Archdiocese of Philadelphia to help me out.

When he suggested that I join the Knights of Columbus

instead, I informed him the Knights were formed after a ban on joining Freemasons was imposed by the Vatican several centuries ago over the battle of separation of Church and State waged in Europe.

I said to him, "Why would I join the second best when I already belong to the best? God will still judge me by my actions and not my memberships. And furthermore my fraternity has never asked me about my religious beliefs nor asked me to choose between Church and the Freemasons. Why should I give in to pressure from my church to make non-religious choices?"

This conversation went on at several levels of the church and eventually resulted in a meeting with the Archbishop trying to get me to join the Knights in place of the Masons. I asked the Archbishop, "How many Masonic Meetings have you attended?"

"Why, none," he replied.

"Well, I've been to many, and I can tell you there is nothing within those meetings that would be in conflict with my Catholic faith."

He pondered for a while and with his hand on my shoulder, said, "I can not condone your actions, but if you feel that strongly about the fraternity then follow your heart."

And I have ever since.

The Line is Cast & the Hook Is In

I was on my way, and I had achieved much. Success was coming my way in large measures. And along with it, came the wink-wink-nod-nod favors gotten and favors returned. I was making regular and highly questionable alliances out of business necessity.

It seems harmless at first, but the adrenaline rush produced by success is highly addictive. There is an ever-increasing need for more of the same. I can tell you from experience, that organized crime harnessed the very same high, drawing the unsuspecting into their world of shady dealings and intimidation. Cut an ethical corner here, sacrifice a principle there; the power derived and influence obtained grows, but so does your list of enemies.

Eventually you turn to those you know who can provide the

protection you need to continue on this road......the very same characters I fell in with at the pool hall—wise guys. You do them certain favors and in turn they reciprocate...slowly building a debt you can *never* escape or repay. Never.

Suddenly, I was "miraculously" being awarded any construction contract I bid on. My contact person came through the immediate family of the local Don, who would ask me for help with some of the properties he controlled. In turn, he would open doors for me in the business world. It proved exciting and extremely profitable.

Before long, I had my own limo with several gun-toting bodyguards on salary. I was also armed to function and survive as an equal in this world of deceit and double cross. I had complete access to the union trades and any license or permits I needed to get an edge over any competitor.

On one occasion, a union representative thought I was putting scabs (non-union workers) to work. He arrived at the job site, came up behind me, and grabbed me by the neck with a hand of steel. I reached for my 9mm and stuck the barrel up against his jugular. Of course, he immediately released his grip, and someone ran up to him and whispered my connection in his ear. He jumped to shake my hand and profusely apologized for the "breach of respect." Still gasping for air, I nodded and moved away.

But the first time I knew I was in too deep was a few years earlier. I went to my Don asking for guidance on a business deal that had gone south. I had been awarded a contract to rehab an abandoned downtown hotel, which was right in the path of a federally funded project linking two major train stations. This hotel would have to be demolished and the price for eminent domain would yield a handsome sales price to the owner. But it didn't take a genius to realize that an operating hotel would fetch a much higher price than an abandoned hotel. So my job was to make this hotel look like an operating business.

One of the principals involved in the deal was a prominent local attorney from a well-known, respected law firm. At the time, the firm was powerful enough to refuse to pay or substantially discount what they owed a vendor and get away with it.

My first invoice to them was thirty-one thousand dollars. They went into the classic stall tactic and I was not amused. Meanwhile my material supplier was pouring on the pressure for payment. I could have gone broke and lost everything. My attorney, who was also a friend, had warned that a lawsuit could be held up in courts for years and there was a good chance that I would never see a dime. When I told him that I'd rather handle the situation myself, he quickly warned me, "Don't tell me anymore. I can't defend you if I know what you did."

No more than 24 hours after I sent out my flare for help, I got a call from my usual contact person and was instructed to show up at a little bar on a back street downtown at eight o'clock the next morning. There I was met by two loyal and persuasive associates known as Artie Slippers and Frankie the Ball, two cartoon-like names, but believe me, they were big, scary, and very real. Their instructions were to do whatever I needed to get the desired result. I explained the situation and the amount owed.

"Fine," said Artie "we'll add five thousand for our side and you keep the balance." I gave the location of the target's office, a few blocks away on the 13th floor.

The plan was simple, they would convince him to pay me in cash and we would go our separate ways, or the attorney would go a "separate way" of his own. This was serious sh-t. We're talking about more than a business favor, and I was now neck-deep. I convinced myself, though, that I was merely an observer and not a player. But my world of self-delusion was ready to come crashing down, and there would be no turning back.

As Artie, Frankie, and I strode toward the office building, it dawned on me that I was about to change my life forever. It seemed five lifetimes had passed since my carefree, pool hall days of running numbers. We walked into the building and looked up the office suite number. We stepped off the elevator, and were greeted by the receptionist. "Good morning, Mr. C," she said, "is Mr. K expecting you?"

"No," I replied, and she politely told us that Mr. K could not see us and we'd need to make an appointment.

Artie smirked and asked, "Where's his office?"

I pointed it out, and Artie Slippers told the receptionist "Don't worry, I'm sure it'll be fine," and we walked into the private office where an obviously annoyed Mr. K quickly hung up the phone and asked what the hell I was doing there.

"He's here to collect what you owe him," Artie said.

Frankie the Ball closed the office door and stood guard, insuring there would be no interruption. Artie walked over and removed a chrome-plated instrument of persuasion from his jacket, assuring him this was no joke.

Mr. K was told to write a check for thirty six thousand dollars to cash, and then call the manager of the bank on the first floor, instructing him to cash the check and put the money in my briefcase.

Artie assured him that he had a choice, either write the check, or the contents of his skull would be spread all over his desk in less than a minute.

He made the call, and I went down to collect the money. They left Mr. K, with his shorts in need of cleaning, and then met me back at the bar to get their split of the money.

Thank God all went as planned. I had never been so scared in my life. I'd been involved in other questionable sh-t, but nothing this serious. I was getting in too deep and I knew it. When my Dad had warned me about these types of guys, he explained how they get you involved, get you on a "long-term lease," and then eventually own you. I received numerous calls from Mr. K, apologizing for the delay in payment, assuring me he had every intention of paying, and that it was all just a misunderstanding. Right.

Mr. K was well hated in the community, due to his arrogant attitude and regular non-payment practices. When word got around that I had played hardball and won, I became the toast of the town.

I started getting calls from people who wanted to do business with the guy who had the balls to put Mr. K in his place. So much work came as a result, that I had to hire more people to keep up. It was a great time for me and no one screwed with me from then on.

The power was going to my head, and things were getting heavy on many levels.

My family had no idea what I did for a living, or with whom I was working. My mother told me she had dreams that kept her up and wanted to know if I was involved with a certain element of people. I knew what she was asking, and assured her I was not. I didn't like lying to my mother but I saw no reason to make her worry.

I had long since drifted from the teachings of my fraternity and the comfort of my faith. Now it was all about money and influence, and I was drunk with its power. Everywhere I went I was shown the respect usually reserved for family members of the powers that controlled the streets. If I wasn't guilty of committing an actual crime, I certainly was by association.

To slow down the crazy pace of that lifestyle and gain a little more control of my destiny, I left Philadelphia and headed for the sleepier streets of the Jersey Shore. I set up a new construction company, bought several building lots with my dad, and began contracting and building duplexes.

I was introduced to a local retired businessman from New York who was a friend of "The Family" that had been asked to look out for me. His name was Charlie and he was well known around town. Everyone knew where he came from, and showed him the respect his connections commanded. Charlie introduced me to his group, and before long I was considered to be his protégé and treated accordingly.

On the first Thursday of every month a dinner was held and attended by well-connected individuals from Philadelphia, New Jersey, New York and Italy, at a restaurant in the center of town. It was known as the Gourmet Club. Anywhere from 60 to 100 guys showed up and engaged in a variety of conversations and problem-solving discussions for hours. Charlie always introduced me as "Don Roberto" which made me nervous. But Charlie assured me it was a sign of respect he felt I had earned.

He introduced me to those he felt could open doors, and cautioned others to stay away from me. He explained that I was a hard-working businessman and not a street operator. It didn't take long for word to spread that I was Charlie's golden boy, and business became another notch easier. Doors were opened that had previously been locked shut. I loved the mode of operation: "Do me this service and someday I will return the favor." It was a beautiful concept of give-and-take, and more effective and efficient than anything I've come across in life thus far. Hard work was the key, but with a little help from Charlie...my bottom line was headed for the sky.

Taking the Bait

"Nothing in life is free...and everything and every person has a price." It might be one of the oldest and truest street survival axioms. But here's another unarguable truth:

Life is a beautiful journey...... truly a gift from our Creator.

But it comes with roadblocks and hurdles, each of which needs to be navigated in order for us to grow.

This belief holds true for both our physical and spiritual well-being. It's easy to convince yourself that by excelling in one area, you can ignore another area. For me, great financial success was in direct opposition to having a shot at establishing a relationship with Christ.

As my notoriety grew, so did my arrogance and my drive for power. I drifted further from the truth and the need to nourish my spiritual being. Some call it a God complex; I call it an ego complex.

I was marching to a lightning-fast drum beat with few warning signs along the way, and no way to roll back the clock and get a second chance to make it right. The only law of survival was to keep moving and have no regrets.

My newfound success brought me cash, but less and less peace of mind. Every night, I essentially slept with one eye open. I would get some sleep, but never woke up to a new day completely rested and refreshed. This was the trade-off for leaving my faith behind.

But there was no trade-off when it came to family. My wife and children were then, and always will be my first priority. My boys were getting older and needed me now more than their mother. The skills they would need in life to survive the streets would have to come from me. I made sure I was there for them, but completely ignoring what I was presenting as an example of manhood. As my boys grew, I slowly began to refocus on what I wanted for them: values, principles, and ideals were at the top of the list and it was up to me to show them the way. I had values, principles, and ideals myself once. I knew how much peace and joy there could be living a life anchored in faith and spirituality.

I traded those away, but I desperately wanted them for my children. The time was coming when I would have to make hard, but obvious choices. I knew it wouldn't be easy getting away from the connections I made, and the obligations I had incurred.

I was thirty-two years old. I had it all: money, cars, property, and power. Whatever we wanted, we could get: reservations, tickets, front row seats to shows and sporting events…the whole shot. My wife asked what this red-carpet treatment was all about, and I told her it was a show of appreciation for favors I had done or gotten done…I explained that it was just a business way of saying thank you. I don't know if she believed me or not, but she never questioned me about it in detail.

The Line Goes Slack

But then the bottom dropped out. In March of that year, the Don was assassinated and war broke out in Philadelphia for control of the rackets and territories. All hell broke loose and things were out of control. Very quickly, almost every connection I had was dead or operating in low profile, survival mode.

I was a non-combatant, and no one cared about me or what I was doing because I had business dealings with a select few, and now they had vanished. I knew the arena I played in wasn't entirely innocent, but I was proficient at convincing myself it was only business. I wasn't naïve, I just had selective memory. But one thing was clear. With many of the players in my drama gone as a result of this mob war, I saw this as the only opportunity I was going to get to turn my life around. This was the time.

I had spent the last ten years making connections and establishing strong relationships at many levels. I no longer needed to prove myself. My reputation was known and alliances fixed. But there was also a list of people who'd have loved to see me in jail. Up until that point, the only thing that stopped them was my protection. With my connections gone, they could conceivably make a move. I guess they thought I was without muscle.

The one thing I learned from the street was that assassins come with an olive branch in one hand and a dagger in the other. It didn't take long until that happened. I received a call from an attorney who was campaign manager for the mayoral candidate in a municipality where I had a large real estate investment. He represented the political party opposite mine, and wanted to meet with me to discuss a possible partnership.

At this point in my life I traveled and conducted business in a custom-made limo to suit my purpose. For privacy, he said he would like to talk in my limo. With a suspicious mind I set up the meeting.

Two days before the meeting I got a call from another attorney I considered a friend. He was the previous solicitor for the same municipality, and up for appointment as a judge. He gave me a cryptic message that went something like this:

"You are going to be set up. The guy who calls you for a meeting will be wearing a wire, and he'll ask you to donate a large amount of cash to his candidate's campaign. The amount asked for would be illegal. And in exchange for this proposed donation, you'll be promised favorable treatment with your land deals when his guy is elected. They want you out of the picture…whatever you do, don't agree to anything. Just tell them you would be glad to donate the legal amount but it would have to be by check."

The meeting went exactly as he described, and I responded exactly as my informant outlined. The plot was confirmed several times afterwards by people I knew and respected. I was happy to see that at least some of my connections had my back.

But that was another warning flag, telling me that I would face more of the same. I realized I had to find my way back to the spiritual place of comfort I once knew. It wasn't going to be easy, but I wanted to get there nonetheless.

I was fighting many battles at that period in my life. Among my adversaries were the U.S. government and the regulatory agencies of New Jersey. It was a stressful time and I was not accustomed to losing. I dug in, fighting the "good" fight. But I later realized it was a battle I could not win. The government had unlimited resources, and the ability to change the rules whenever they were behind. I hadn't yet learned how to control my arrogance, bullheadedness, and the 'screw you' mentality I previously enjoyed while under the protection of my associates. They were gone now, and this was the federal government.[1]

But growing up around the element I did, surrender was never an option and so I paid the price for my pride and kept on fighting anyway. It cost me a great deal…in money and in emotional wear and tear. I should have put my ego aside and listened to my wife who begged me to stop the seemingly endless challenges and appeals of court decisions.

Through all of this, my family, especially my wife, stood by me and never said, "I told you so." My Dad, whose respect and approval I sought, and took years to earn, was now in jeopardy. He watched me grow from a street kid, to college grad, to family man, and successful businessman. He was proud, but disliked my attitude. He was not aware of all that was going on in my life and my methods were not his. I told him many times that the world he grew up in no longer existed. "Today," I would tell him, "your word and your handshake mean nothing. People will screw you for an extra dollar."

"You might be right" he said, "but you should never let anyone know how smart you really are." A precaution I had practiced at one point, but felt I no longer needed, since I had protection.

---

[1] *The details of that war of nerves are in the many law journals documenting my landmark wetlands case from 1983 to 1986, listed as United States v. Ciampitti*

He stood by me through those days, but once in awhile I could see the sadness in his eyes. I guess he thought after all those years I would have finally learned who he really was, and would learn from what he had accomplished.

Every so often I would reflect back on something my Grandfather told me when I was an overconfident teenager. "Bobby", he told me,

"God put his only son Jesus on this earth to show us the way. He walked the earth for thirty-three years and after that time, they crucified and killed him. The next day the sun still came up. You're not that important."

After four years of fighting a legal battle, and 1.5 million dollars later, I was pretty banged up but not beaten. I learned from the experience and survived to fight another day.

Slowly, I became less arrogant and indifferent. By opening my heart to those around me, I was learning how it felt to exist in a world of tolerance and compassion.

My sons were involved in sports and scouting, and I was committed to share in their experiences. I saw promise and hope in their eyes everyday. My relationship with my wife became less tumultuous, and peace and spirituality were finding their way into my life once again.

I was clearly on a new path. It would take time to find Christ and the Church again, but felt that the God I was reacquainting myself with, would be patient with me.

Of course, my habits of the past would cause me to stumble occasionally. I would pick myself up again and again, and try once more with family as my inspiration. I kept close to my sons to prevent them from falling into the same traps I had. I was adamant in encouraging them to choose a career path not riddled with temptation.

One chose law, and the other engineering. I always felt God was watching over me and protecting my family. The more control I've been able to release in God's capable hands, the more gifts he bestows upon us.

One Step Forward – Two Steps Back

I spent five years restructuring my business and personal life. I was happy and looking forward to a new future of promise and growth.

My wife and I had made plans on how we could enjoy life uncluttered by obligation and necessity. Our sons were in college and had become fine young men with their own lives to live and enjoy.

But the bright future was not so bright. The economy was beginning to turn. It didn't look pretty, so I began setting a strategy to protect what I had achieved to keep my family safe and financially secure. What I thought was self-preservation led me straight back to my old style of thinking and feeling. My economic woes led me to pursue my former "kill or be killed" style. I categorized the people who were actively or unwittingly kicking me while I was struggling to survive, as my enemies; and eventually abandoned anything you might call Christian behavior. I didn't care who got hurt. It was either them or me, and I always picked me.

As they came up, I recognized those all too familiar negative emotions welling up inside me. I knew how dangerous and vindictive I could be if pushed too far...but I had it rationalized as a matter of self-preservation.

I was determined to deal with my "enemies" in the cruelest manner possible once the crises passed. My buddy, the attorney, was always fond of saying, "*Revenge is a dish best served cold.*" I was nasty enough to totally embrace that completely un-Christian concept and looked forward to paying back enemies. Some of whom didn't even know they were on my list. The plan I would expedite over the next few years would destroy them, socially, financially and emotionally. I successfully orchestrated their complete life breakdown.

I look back at the emotional carnage I was responsible for and am truly saddened. I know now that I'd been deluding myself, thinking I was only doing what needed to be done, but I knew there were many better paths to take. I also knew that my continuation of that old school, revenge, power-is-everything pattern would kill me if I let it continue. I wanted to make a new start.

I was still a member of the Masons Fraternity, but not active. A friend of my eldest son, Brad, called and asked if I would talk to him about the Freemasons. He had been reading about the fraternity, knew I was a member, and wanted some insight. Over a two-week period we discussed many of the institution's teachings and precepts. He asked if I would sponsor him for initiation. I agreed and went with him to meet some of the members of the lodge. His excitement reminded me why I joined the fraternity in the first place and motivated me, once again, to become an active member in my lodge.

That one small decision reopened my mind and heart, reminding me what impact a man can have on others by simply holding himself to a higher standard and always trying to do the right thing...not necessarily the easy thing.

I was drawn in and nurtured once again by many of my Masonic Brothers. Their encouragement and support caused me to move ahead in my lodge, and it was both demanding and rewarding. I began to grow in a number of ways but most importantly, in ways which were spiritually uplifting.

I was elected to the office of Junior Warden, then Senior Warden and finally I became Worshipful Master of the Lodge, a title of respect taken from Old English society.

During that time, I visited many other lodges here and abroad. No matter which country I visited, I was always greeted and taken in with the utmost hospitality and lack of pre-judgment. I learned many new things about the fraternity and new things about myself. Meeting with many groups and giving numerous talks on the ideals of the Masonic Fraternity was inspirational and allowed me to meet many men who could relate to me, and were searching for meaning in their lives.

The Grand Lodge of Pennsylvania called upon me for help and I was appointed to the high office of District Deputy Grand Master. In the Masonic world, this is an honorable position with many trappings, benefits and responsibilities. Seven Masonic Lodges were put under my authority consisting of over two thousand members. All matters of a Masonic nature are to be directed to the District Deputy for council and resolution and his decision is autonomous and final. When given that kind of authority, you act and react more cautiously, employing fairness, justice and equity in everything.

Those demands made me a better person, more reflective, and even more spiritual. Men approached me with all types of issues and concerns. Although my obligation was limited to Masonic issues, my affection for my brothers pushed me to do whatever I could to help on a wide selection of issues - marital, medical, financial, religious, or family related. It was almost like being their confessor. My opinion on virtually anything had meaning and it was a heavy weight of responsibility to bear.

Snapping the Line to Swim Free

I received a call from a Jersey Shore friend and business associate. He told me he had given my name and phone number to a commercial real estate developer. It seems that this guy was planning on making a major investment in the township where I had a great deal of experience and connections. After a lengthy phone conversation about his project, we arranged to meet face to face and develop a strategy to help his cause.

The meeting was pleasurable and informative. We became instant friends and soon found ourselves in several partnerships together. Aside from our mutual business interests, we had personal similarities as well.

I can't remember how the topic came up, but we began to talk at length about the Masonic Fraternity and my long association with that brotherhood.

Intrigued, he asked if I could set up a private tour of the Masonic Temple at One North Broad Street in Philadelphia, the home of the Grand Lodge of Pennsylvania.

That tour made an impact on him and his curiosity about the Freemasons grew. After his tour, we went to lunch and I was stunned when he reached across the table as our food was delivered and said, "Bobby, lets give thanks to God bringing us together." Reaching across the table he grabbed my hands and said, "He must have a plan for us and He will open our hearts to new challenges."

I had an image and a reputation to uphold in this town, and thought to myself, "This isn't what others would expect me to do in public." I was known as a tough guy with connections, and ability to get things done. Not that I was embarrassed by my Christian beliefs, but it was something I kept to myself. So this was completely new ground for me. I was impressed, however, that a man of his stature would be so comfortable with such a public display of his faith and devotion. So I joined hands for the prayer.

Now, *I* was curious about *him*. Later that day he explained to me that he hosted a weekly reflection group of men at his office and invited me to join. He felt I had something to offer and maybe I would get something out of it. I told him I would think about it and thanked him for the consideration and concern for my spiritual well being.

Not sure if this was something I wanted to participate in, I put it off for months. He continued to invite me to each meeting and I didn't want to offend him. I respected this man and he was helping me in areas not business related, and reciprocation was both warranted and deserved.

I attended what would turn out to be one of many reflection group meetings yet to come.

I sat and listened to men whose sole purpose was to share feelings and experiences in their lives, and attempt to bolster their faith and grow spiritually.

It reminded me of what my Masonic beliefs were and how closely they paralleled the Christian principles being discussed. After a few meetings I began to participate and share some of my thoughts and observations about the scripture passage being read.

My friend, and chairman of this group told me how much he and others appreciated my insights, and how I brought a realistic and ground level aspect to the table.

They began to refer to me as the curb height apostle (an apostle, but at the lowest level). It was funny but true. I seemed to have an innate ability to find the quickest way to analyze a conversation, and reduce it to its lowest common denominator. It was a valued tool in my life, and I applied it here as well.

Here I Am Lord

And now, here I am, firm in my convictions yet receptive to ideas and opinions of others. Now secure in my beliefs, and once again, keenly aware of my Catholic faith. Still not committed to the ritual of attending Church on a weekly basis, but confident my relationship with God is sound.

I will be ready. I will share the light with others, and when my time finally comes I will close my eyes with the peace knowing I have done my best, and surrender my soul to my Creator in confidence.

Everything in life happens for a reason. I repressed my thoughts and actions for decades until now. I was destined to make the choices I did, and endure the experiences generated by those choices. But life and our contact with others is greatly affected by "The Domino Effect." Once the first piece is pushed, there is no control over what piece will fall next, or what direction they will fall. Just one change in my past would have produced a different outcome and change my current place in life. If you don't like where you are in life and you want to "take it over"................ think again. God has given us free will, but our destiny is predetermined. *All we can change is how we get there and how much good or evil we expel along the way.*

We can, and now I will, have a heightened sense of voluntary action. I still expect to fail on occasion, but I hope to make better decisions in the process.

Temptations are a gift from God. What I mean is, by experiencing temptations, we build up spiritual antibodies to fight off larger and more destructive temptations that will inevitably confront us. There can be no testimony without a test.

There are many issues I am currently dealing with which must be resolved, mostly of a business nature but stressful nonetheless. With my renewed connection to God I can now find peace and strength to get through life's many adversities without resorting to "the old me." I am comforted, knowing God is always at my side and when I need him, He always answers. I am never alone in the company of the one who will never let me down.

From my own experience, I can assure you that being honest with yourself and following the voice of your heart will surely lead you to Jesus Christ's front door.

I can also tell you it is never too late to turn your life around. In the end, good will always prevail because your judgment day will be handled by your Creator, and the witness to your actions will be your conscience.

With support of my family and God's help, I hope to maintain the direction I have outlined here. Only time will tell how successful I will be or how many times I may fail.

But I have learned and believe that my God is a temperate and forgiving God. He sits with me everywhere I go and will come to my aid in the fight against evil; all we have to do, is ask.

Pray for me as I continue to do my utmost to reach my goals and hopefully, in a positive way, touch the lives of others.

Bob Campitti

The Addict

Harry Allen

Every Step You Take

My life began as a spoiled rotten kid. I was one of the lucky ones, living the American dream; in our case, the African-American dream. I just didn't know how lucky I was. I would waste over a quarter million dollars on drugs, waste a good portion of my life, and throw all that good luck away.

My grandfather sold produce and pork products (ham hocks, chitterlings, hog maws, pig knuckles, neck bones, fat back and the like) from the back of a pick-up truck. He did well. People liked him and what he was selling – just that simple. His success allowed him to open a small store out of his house, and that quickly led to him opening a legitimate grocery store. It was the first-ever Negro supermarket in America. Yes, that's the word that made the newspapers before it was considered wrong to use. Ebony magazine did a feature story on it, and amongst photos of my granddad, grandmother, dad, mom, uncles and aunts, you can pick out a six year old me.

I guess, looking back, I was just plain bad. I got spanked almost every day and deserved it. I stole money from my father whenever he'd leave his wallet on the bureau. I would take a few dollars, and go buy breakfast at a diner around the corner from my house. The food wasn't necessarily that good; I just did it because I could, figuring I deserved to have whatever I wanted, whenever I wanted.

By the age of 12, I was 5 feet 10 inches. I became too headstrong and mule-stubborn; as a result, ended up in an all-black, Catholic military school 40 miles west of Richmond, Virginia. We were rousted out of our cots at 5:55 every morning, and at 6:20 am we had our choice of going to study hall or attending Mass at the school church. I chose Mass and rose in the ranks to become an altar boy. Not that I liked it all that much…but it got me away from the grind of marching.

That first Christmas break, I caught my father sneaking out of the house late one night, and it wasn't long before my parents were divorced. My dad was a hard-working, basically good man who enjoyed bowling, golf and all kinds of sports, but the sport he enjoyed most was chasing the ladies. That seemed to me to be his only weakness. He was a professional skirt chaser and I was destined to follow in his footsteps.

Back at military school, I ruled the roost in any kind of card game. I was smart, and topped 1400 on my SAT's. But most notably, I secured an academic scholarship to Notre Dame.

At 16 though, I wanted to go to a college with more female scenery. Michigan State was my ticket, and in my first semester I majored in Party Time and was intent on attending every party on campus. I flunked out before the first semester's grades were even submitted. I could have been the first in my family to go to college. But, Notre Dame—I ignored it. Michigan State—I blew it.

A Working Man

From the age of eight, I had always worked in the family store. Now I was working in the family business at 19 with my own apartment. I thought I was a man, and as such I figured it was my right to do as I pleased. That meant when my workday was done, I had the right to get high and party all night long. I was free. At least I thought that was freedom.

I was at the right place at the right time since my family was opening a new store in the big city…and was going to be one of four family owners. Three years into the new store, we were making sinful money and I was busy following my father's woman-chasing ways. Whenever a fine woman would come in to cash a check…I would hit on her like a ton of bricks and my batting average was pretty good. I was carving notch after notch in my belt (after all, it was the seventies). Free love, free will. I was what they called a player. I lived in the right part of the suburbs, versus the hood. I drove a new model car every year. I was working 80 hours a week, but I was making money hand over fist. I thought I was god and life was good...very good.

But working those hours and being a 'player,' I needed something to keep me going. I convinced my doc to write scrips for black beauties (uppers). So what got me up every morning was a few black beauties and my mandatory cup of coffee. What put me to sleep every night was high-grade marijuana. It was my first drug combination crutch.

Problem, no problem. I just needed a *little* something to help. I would find out later it's the *little* things...that become too big to handle.

"Money Changes Everything"

Money did change everything. The more money we made at the store, the more attention (both good and bad) it attracted. One day a drug addict came into the store, pulled a .38 on me, and said, "Give me the money!" I found myself in a trance floating above the entire scene looking down on me and the drug addict with his gun. I was hovering like a spirit.

I was very calm and continued to say to the robber, "Here's the money, take the money and run." Shots ended up being fired outside, but the only thing I remember was hovering over the scene, watching like some kind of detached spirit. I felt that God had blessed me and allowed me to escape being shot by a drug addict. I had no idea that just a short time later, it would be me waving the gun in someone's face, holding up a store, too stoned to care.

My player lifestyle continued on for the next three years, and I slept with every woman possible from Michigan to California and back. My father and I went into the check cashing business, and in the course of things, I met an actress who introduced me to another 'actress' I'll just refer to her as Ms. Cocaine. She told me that on cocaine, our sex would be 10 times greater and told me the things we would do. I was in. I tried mescaline on my 21st birthday, but the high of cocaine had me hooked from the very first try.

Between my raging nightlife and my heavy load of hours at work, sleep became a low priority. By now the coke or the 'caine, as some called it, wasn't just a way to make it through the day without sleep; it gave me what I thought was a lifestyle. That life included hanging out with other users. One night one of the crew named "Doc" asked me if I had ever "free-based." I told him no, and he said, "Why not try some?"

Why Not?

Those two words: why not? Those two words sent my life into a living hell for the next ten years.

Doc took some stony looking stuff and put it on a clear pipe. He dipped a hanger with a piece of cotton on the end into 151-proof rum, lit the cotton and put it into the hole of the clear pipe inhaling deeply.

On my first try, nothing happened. He said that sometimes you had to try it a couple of times. I tried it again and he was right. I was "free-basing", but as I learned the hard way, over the next 10 years, there was absolutely nothing free about it.

After that hit, hardly a day went by that I didn't free-base. The physical addiction was instant. This was a habit I had no chance of shaking. At first, I could handle the cost for what I used, but that would eventually change.

It seemed like I was out to set a record for how many mistakes I could make and still live. I got married while still addicted to free-basing. Being married didn't slow my sport of chasing women in the slightest. One of the major ways I was affected by coke was sexual; when I was loaded I came up with some truly freaky stuff. Many partners and even three-way sex—were a regular occurrence. I, the married guy, chased dope and women daily.

Just like in every drug addict story you've ever heard, when the money got short, I started stealing to buy more dope. I stole the money from our check-cashing business (my father's and mine), telling myself that I would pay it all back at some point and that I was just "borrowing."

Crossing the Line

I landed another day job at a competitor's check cashing shop, still getting high, still partying non-stop. At the end of a typical two-day drug run, I blabbed to my buddy that there was $30,000 cash in the safe at work.

Completely strung out, I immediately got to thinking we could set up a fake robbery...then use the money to buy more cocaine, and then start dealing to support our habit. At 3 am, after no sleep for two days, this sounded like a real master-stroke and what's really weird is that it actually made sense to me! I was able to convince my partner that it would be a practical solution to our money problems.

So the next day, my buddy came in and "robbed me." At first, it looked like the scam was going to work, but I hadn't counted on the police giving me a lie-detector test. I guess I wasn't too shocked when they told me my results weren't so great. I'd been in jail before and I'd watched enough crime TV to know that you're never supposed to talk to the police, but somehow I thought the moment was right to spill everything. When I got to court, I pleaded out with simple burglary. I was ready to do some serious time but the jail cells were so full that I got probation, and not a day's worth of prison. There was a message for me somewhere. I just wasn't receiving. Some part of me was sick of going down the wrong road and just wanted to confess. But when I got a pass, there was probably another part of me that thought I was too cool for jail.

My next job was working for Electronic Data Systems. After being there just a few months, a co-worker asked if I could help pull a fake car theft so he could get the insurance money. My partner in crime from the failed $30,000 robbery was ready for anything to support our habit, and this was right up our alley. But the guy collecting the insurance got caught, and flipped on us.

This time there was no slick lawyer, only a Public Defender who told me to take a plea. He said I could get six years in prison, but if I took a plea of six months in prison and six months in rehab, we wouldn't go to trial (which had a 95% conviction rate). I took the deal.

I now know that God had blessed me right then and there……….. but I was still running from him.

After surviving six months in prison, I was shipped off to rehab. I was amazed at the amount of B.S. being thrown around in the group rehab meetings. Pretty much everyone was flat-out lying about everything they had ever done or intended to do. The "highly trained" therapists or psychologists believed every bit of it. But therapists, or anyone without experience in real addiction can't have the slightest idea about what addiction is all about. It takes one to know one. No textbook can *ever* describe the stranglehold you experience when you're addicted.

Out of rehab, I bounced between living with friends and ex-girlfriends…ending up in a burned-out apartment without water or electricity. With no place to go, I reached out to the one lifeline I could think of.

One Good Man Is All It Takes

During my six months in prison, a cousin from Atlanta, Georgia had written me and told me not to lose hope and hang in there. He invited me to come stay with him when I got out, when I was serious about giving up the low life. He offered to help me in any way he could. I thanked him and had immediately thrown his number in the trash. The idea of living the "straight life" was beyond my imagination at the time. But now, with nowhere to go, he was my last resort. I found his number, made the call, and asked him if the offer was still good.

He assured me that I would be more than welcome. My grandmother and mother's girlfriend took me downtown to get a suit, a couple of shirts, and pair of pants at the Salvation Army. On the 14th of June, I boarded a bus headed to Atlanta. I had already made up my mind to do the right thing, but I was still thinking like a junky. I had gotten high on my last little stash of crack earlier that day. I arrived in Atlanta, Georgia on the 15th of June and no longer had a desire to get high…no desire at all. God's blessing.

Upon arrival, my cousin set down the rules. No drugs……and I had to attend *church*, every Sunday, with their family. I settled into my new life, and after two weeks, a church Sunday school teacher suggested I go to a Bill Gotherd seminar, which ran four-days. I remember that Friday evening like it was yesterday. For years I'd been hearing the phrase, "Jesus died for our sins." But I had never really understood. That night it became clear. I took an inventory of all of the sins I had committed, and it finally dawned on me. He died for me. I broke down and sobbed. It was June 30; the day God bestowed his eternal blessing on my life.

The following Sunday I went to church and told the pastor I had been saved, and wanted to be baptized. The next Sunday, I walked down the church aisle a changed man. I was still wearing my Salvation Army excuse for a suit but had a Detroit glide in my stride. This heathen was about to be baptized. If it could happen to someone who had stolen, whored, and done more than a quarter million dollars worth of drugs; it could happen to anyone. The people sitting there that day knew I was now one of them, ready to serve the Lord.

God was in my life, and now, I was ready to listen.

My cousin told me I should be looking for a job, and that was no easy task for a man with a prison record. I started praying to the Lord for a job and my prayers were answered. I wasn't offered one job, I was offered three. They were simple minimum wage jobs, but since I hadn't worked for more than a year, it felt great to be doing something.

If You Are Faithful in Small Things, God Will Trust You with Larger Things

Within a year, I was hired as an assistant manager in a local supermarket. Then a better job followed; a guy from church asked if I thought I could be a salesman. Reviewing my life experience and my street smarts, I was pretty sure I could sell snow to an Eskimo, so I filled out the application. I skipped the felony ques-tion, interviewed for the job, and became a salesman for a Fortune

500 company with a company car, expense account...the works. I quickly became the Number One salesman in my region, regularly breaking monthly sales records.

Work filled me up, but there was still a hole in my soul. I had gotten to the place in my life where I was missing the love of a good woman. That missing part of my soul was close at hand. I met a wonderful woman while we were both picking up product at a wholesaler and struck up a conversation. We sat and prayed together in church for eight years. Our long friendship, and then courtship, led to marriage. My happiness was unstoppable. I had become a Deacon, and led a ministry dealing with addiction. I even sang solo parts in the choir. I had found faith at last.

But one day I heard my pastor say something in a meeting that wasn't true. I had to call him on it, and he instantly turned on me, accusing *me* of being the liar. He never took back what he said, and I found it impossible to serve under him knowing he was a false prophet--and an unrepentant one.

The church I loved, the church I found...had it all been a dream? Had it all been false? Something like this could swing people away from faith like a hurricane destroying the home you lived in for many years, but God loved me. I loved Him. My faith in a church had been rocked, but my faith in God wasn't. Looking for another church was difficult but I found one, and once again, I was able to believe. I poured every bit of my love and energy into my new place of worship and its congregation.

But the second church I attended for years was not the right fit either. That church pretty much dictated that I was going to die in sin, and go straight to hell...but I knew God to be 100% about forgiveness. And with my past, I needed that forgiveness. I was walking with the Lord, but walking into the wrong church.

For the second time, my faith in a church was rocked, but my faith in God wasn't. I was simply wearing a shirt that didn't fit... but I wasn't about to stop wearing shirts.

So again, I asked my wife if she would be OK with seeking a different place of worship, and she, along with my mom and her mom, reluctantly started going with me to a third church.

There are many churches in this world, and sometimes the first one you try…or the second one you try, won't be the one that fits. But just like shirts, some fit and some don't, but you can't give up wearing shirts altogether just because the first few don't fit you. It's the same with faith…it may take a few churches to find the one that fits you.

Where am I now? I'm Home…..Home with the Lord.

I found a pastor who believes in love, and not so much in rules.

My pastor is a little crazy, but his love of the Lord is undeniable. Hearing him speak, you can feel his life commitment. I'm blessed to have found a church of love and sensitivity.

As I look back on the 40 years of my life as an addict, I am so grateful to God, who always had my back even when I refused to know Him…..even as I kept running away from Him. He never gave up on the hopeless drug mess and whore that I was. He was always there, waiting for me to say "OK…Now. I'm ready now."

When I lived with my grandmother in early boyhood she would always pray for me. She prayed for me to be saved from fighting in the Vietnam War. She prayed me away from the sickness of drugs. Someone somewhere has prayed for *you* or is praying for you *right now*. And <u>that prayer will last forever</u>. No one can take away that prayer.

I came to Atlanta on a bus with nothing but Salvation Army clothes on my back. Because I said "Now" to the Lord, and was faithful in the small things, I now have all I that I need to live a rich and full life.

Today, I'm involved in jail ministry and our church's addiction ministry (takes one to know one). I'm leading the men's ministry, and my wife and I are care pastors for over 30 families.

I love the Lord. He saved me and He loves me. It's an eternal love, and I marvel how He has changed a man like me for the better. But it's not really a mystery…all I had to do was say, "Now."

Thank you, Lord, thank you.

HARRY ALLEN

The Cancer Patient

Todd Painton

Looking Down From Above

I was four years old. I remember it being one of those beautiful sunlit days. It was a summertime golf outing and picnic. While the fathers were out pretending to be pros on the greens, the kids and moms were playing and relaxing by the pool. Somehow, I escaped the safety of my mother's arms, and ran full speed towards the baby pool. I lost my footing, slipped backwards, and hit my head.

Everything went quiet. I felt no pain...no sensation at all. Then I remember somehow floating in air, hovering above the entire scene. I could see my mother in a panic, picking me up and carrying me over to the nearest chair. A crowd pressed in around her, and with my bird's eye view, I could see golf carts darting across the fairways, and cars driving by. Someone was with me, holding me quietly. There were no words spoken, but I distinctly remember quietly saying, "Yes. Yes, I will remember."

Then I floated gracefully back down to the concrete apron of the pool, into the chair, and back into my mother's arms. The total silence gradually disappeared, and the sounds of life returned to a full-volume roar.

I let out a cry, and the pain from the lump on my head mingled with the warmth of the sun and tears on my face. The rest of the afternoon was spent playing quietly and avoiding the baby pool.

Once again, at age five, I was lifted into the air and was looking down on another scene - myself, my family, and friends in our backyard. The same presence held me, but it seemed to be more than one. I was shown something that I've never been allowed to remember, but I was compelled to make that same quiet commitment, "I will not forget, I promise."

I was born with a missing bone from my inner ear, so my hearing was weak and scar tissue had built up from numerous ear infections as a baby. Being spoken to without hearing any specific words... fluctuations in sound ... inner conversations ... all seemed normal to me.

The movie reel of my childhood played on. We moved to the East coast, and I had the chance to fall in love with the Chesapeake Bay, creating my own version of a Huckleberry Finn lifestyle. Bare feet along the waterways, hours of fishing adventures, spending more time in boats than cars, and a selection of endless sunsets were all permanently etched into my memory banks. But this was also a time when I first met real pain head-on.

It was there that I experienced the pain of child abuse. Just as the studies say: it was perpetrated by someone close to our family, in the form of inappropriate, and sometimes sexual, behavior. Other members of my family were abused as well, and we reacted in individual but equally painful ways. It was during those years I was also exposed to pornography, which set a dark precedent for my relationships with women later in life.

From fourth grade to sixth grade, we moved three times with the twists and turns of my father's career. As I think back on it now, he was most likely a victim of depression. By the time we had settled down, I turned eleven and my legs had begun to give me trouble. Over the next year, swelling made my knees the size of softballs, and I went to the doctor every two weeks to have them drained.

I was diagnosed with juvenile rheumatoid arthritis, was on leg immobilizers, and walked only with the aid of crutches. My mother spoke to the doctor and asked about my chances of ever running or playing sports again. His reply was that running was not very likely, and he then advised our focus should be limited to walking.

My mother told the doctor his answer was unacceptable,

grabbed my hand, and stormed out of the office. She made an appointment with another specialist. After blood tests, taking note of some rashes I had gotten that summer, the new doctor accurately diagnosed me with Lyme disease.

This... after two years of countless procedures, and draining gallons of yellow, bloody fluid from my knees. According to Children's Hospital of Pennsylvania, I was one of the first documented pediatric cases on the east coast, and my case was presented at a national medical conference in California in 1984 – not exactly what I would've hoped to be famous for.

After several weeks in the hospital on an intravenous penicillin drip, the swelling cleared, the pain was gone, and I went home.

But when I ran, even for short bursts, my knees would lock up in pain and I would fall to the ground. Three separate surgeries were required to clean out and repair cartilage damage in both knees. After the last surgery, at 15, I tried out for the soccer team after being discharged from the hospital a few days prior. We had to run a mile as part of tryouts, and I finished dead last, but I finished. The coach told me how much he admired my efforts, but I wasn't going to make the team.

That same school year, I had a huge growth spurt. All of a sudden, I was one of the tallest kids in my class. I thought, "Basketball...that might be the way to go." My entire junior year, I threw myself into working out, getting into shape, and taking my frustrations out on the basketball court.

I was fueled by the doctor who told me to forget about running. I was propelled by the anger and rage of an innocent child abused. By the end of my senior year, I gained enough attention from college scouts to be offered a scholarship to play at a Division II school. Before I finished high school I underwent two more surgeries...one to address the deafness in my ear, and one for a lesion in my right eye. I fought through every obstacle thrown my way.

Beneath all that aggressive fighting spirit was a sense that I always had something to prove. My level of intensity had built to a boiling point - allowing me to win great praise on the court, but causing problems everywhere else. I found myself involved in hot-tempered relationships, either with friends, or with girls. Attaining or maintaining any semblance of peace or serenity was beyond reach. There was a drive inside of me that kept everyone on edge. My heart had two speeds: redline and full stop. I had no relationship with God because in my mind, it was me against the world.

Once thrown into the college scene, my inner drive and conflict played out in full color. What served me so well on the court drove me towards dangerous behavior off the court.

Athletically, I caught a few breaks and the coach announced that I would start at power forward my freshman year. My four-year career culminated in over 1000 points scored, winning a conference championship, and being voted University Male Athlete of the Year. The team and I were inducted into the school's Hall of Fame. And of course, with all that praise and prowess came the benefits off-court. I took full advantage.

Once college was over, I was exhausted. Without basketball, over-the-top intensity and inner conflict had no worthwhile place in my life. I was bored and lost, certainly not the best mind set to bring to any relationship. I had a girl who meant a lot to me back in my second year of college, but was in no position to think about getting serious or settling down. Our relationship consisted of chaos and intensity, the only kind of relationship I knew how to have, and continued a roller coaster pattern of on-and-off dating for the next several years.

Struggling to find the right career, I tried a first year of law school but the party life was far more interesting than torts. Before the end of my first year, my girlfriend and I took a trip to Colorado. It only took a 15-minute conversation on the plane home for us to decide I would quit law school, we would get married, and move West.

We were the poster children for how not to approach a marriage. I had no job and we'd only been back together a few months before getting engaged. All of our family and friends thought we were nuts. They had it right.

Our honeymoon was contemptuous, and I realized we'd made a huge mistake. But we stuck with it, loaded up the truck and headed to Denver. Predictably, after six months, I moved out. The trauma of being alone and away from home took its toll on my wife.

And slowly...very slowly...God started to work his way into my life. Now living on my own, I began to have very tangible experiences with Him.

I was working for a construction company, and after all of the leg problems and growth spurts from childhood, my right leg was a full one-inch shorter than my left. Now, that shorter leg was causing me tremendous back pain.

One of my customers invited me to his church on Sunday, and asked if I wanted to be "prayed over" for healing. I was sure this was simply some kind of well-meaning religious tradition, but desperate to relieve my pain, I accepted his invitation. In the basement of a small, plain church building located out near the county line, I was anointed with oil by a humble and friendly group of elders. Unfamiliar prayers were recited.

I felt a force enter the top of my head, move down through my entire body, and exit through my feet. My teeth shifted, my lungs filled up with air, and my legs moved. God's Holy Spirit had come upon me.

Back in Denver, I asked my chiropractor to re-measure my legs. I made sure *not* to tell him about my healing session. After several measurings he told me, with a truly puzzled look on his face, that my legs were now the same exact length. I then shared my Holy Spirit experience and he was convinced that what had happened to me was real.

God started putting friends in my life that had faith, and were loving. I began going to church on my own, not knowing what to do, but feeling that's where I needed to be. The guilt of abandoning my marriage was becoming clear. I approached Susie about reconciling time and again, but I had no real plan as to how to make the marriage work.

For the next five years, we would get back together as husband and wife and then separate while moving back and forth across the country. I was aware that my relationship with God was beginning to slowly grow.

I was exposed to Bible study and the baptisms of the Holy Spirit for the first time. You can't imagine my surprise when, out of nowhere, I started to pray in tongues. After learning about the epic battle for souls between "the enemy" and God, I was at full attention for the first time since leaving the college locker room. At 27, I wanted to do something for God full-time, to be part of the most important team of all.

But I had a crumbling marriage, and if I couldn't handle that, how could I handle the rest of the world? By now, Susie had moved east, leaving me to figure out my next move. That move presented itself when the head coaches from my college invited me to help coach a new team. I thought this could be my chance: I could coach and teach, while getting my feet back on the ground - finally finding my missing stability. Susie saw the same opportunity for us and we moved in together on campus. But true to form, after a year, we split again. I was sure this time it was for good. I thought I was facing reality by hiring a divorce lawyer.

During the beginning stages of the divorce process, I outlined my plan to a man I trusted, and he said something that stopped me cold in my tracks. He said simply and plainly, "Your first ministry is to your wife, nothing you do will be blessed until you resolve this in your life."

It was a painful truth to accept. The words just wouldn't stop echoing inside my head...like church bells that never stopped ringing.

I hopped in my Toyota pickup truck and drove two days straight to see Susie. It was daytime when I got there, and went directly to her office. I walked right into her office and blurted out, "You've got every right to divorce me, and I'll understand if you do. Until I become the man and husband God is calling me to be, I don't want to give up on us, and I haven't done that yet."

She looked at me with those big knowing eyes of hers, shrugged her shoulders, and was speechless. We continued on as husband and wife. Our problems didn't end, and there were times I wanted to leave yet again, but God told me to stand still.

Stillness...a concept I always had trouble relating to and a state I could rarely achieve. I couldn't be still with myself...or be still with anyone. But God was teaching me forgiveness, and began chipping away at my impulsiveness. *Wait. Pause. Don't act just yet. Be patient in adversity.*

I ran away from this relationship for years—I was hiding. But now...now I didn't want to run anymore. And with that understood, I would have to face the discomfort of my own internal struggles. Hearing the details of my own inner pains, past and present, screeching like nails down a schoolhouse chalkboard. I would have to face myself and face the relationships that I could either contribute to or destroy. It was time to purge the darkness from my soul, and the pains of my past, one by one. I vowed to stay and take a long, hard look at my own ugly demons. Endurance would be the key. I'd just keep showing up every day.

For years, I had been running away from reality. Now I was standing my ground and facing my life head-on and it began to bring peace, and for me, that feeling of stillness. Susie and I were blessed with four children in five years, Luke, Jacob, Sarah, and Hannah, who continue to be evidence there can be heaven right here on earth. I became a successful salesman in the construction industry by making constant and solid efforts to understand people and by trying to love my brothers and sisters in this life just as God loves each and every one of us.

But just as I started to see some light, God brought on the darkest of nights. He obviously had other plans for me. While driving home from work one evening, I rubbed my eye and felt a lump. I woke up a few days later with a pool of blood in my right eye. The doctors cut open the lump, and after testing the white cauliflower substance, I was diagnosed with ocular melanoma... cancer of the eye.

A tumor the size of a quarter resting on my eyeball was removed. We were scared, and the everyday nonsense that seemed so big...now looked tiny, in comparison to the threat of cancer.

In my fear, God drew me close to him. I spent a lot of time alone, keeping journals and chronicling the graces that he blessed us with daily. He helped develop discipline and peace in my spirit. He showed me the redemptive value of suffering, and what His son endured for all of us.

One summer night, I sat in adoration and praise of Him, and then I saw Him. Jesus was walking towards me, between two large trees in a garden. A bright light was shining between the two trees, with vibrant green vines all around Him. He motioned to me with a warm, faint smile. He moved His hand towards me, and motioned to follow Him back into the light. He turned and walked in. And suddenly, the vision was over.

After a solid year of biopsies, radiation, and follow-ups, we thought the cancer was in remission, but no such luck. Three weeks after my vision of Jesus, the cancer in my eye had returned. Two more surgeries came, a total of nine surgeries in 18 months. Then...the cancer spread from my eye, to my neck, and then to my liver.

I am currently diagnosed with stage four metastatic melanoma, and am undergoing chemotherapy as I write. Odds have been placed on the treatment's success, as well as my living or dying. The proverbial point-spread of life...it changes things when you *know* your own point-spread and that knowledge has created a new season in my life.

Jesus has invited me into a special place of friendship with Him, to share my small suffering with His suffering. I've been given the grace to realize something amazing about suffering which is this: God could've showed Himself *any* way He wanted. His choice...was to give us His son, and show Himself through suffering, sending His power across time and space. I'm learning now, just how much power there is in suffering.

In a strange way, I have more hope *now* than ever before. I've been able to do this by shifting my focus from finding all the faults in life, to embracing each new day with both feet firmly planted on the ground. God has shown me the depths of darkness and pain. He's also shown me how I've been distant from Him. He has reached out to me and like a small child in an unfamiliar and scary place...I hold His hand tightly and feel safer in his gentle presence. My prayer life is rich, and I dream about the vapors of my prayers floating up before His altar and throne in Heaven, to be answered according to His will.

God is teaching me the difference between false humility and hiding from His call. As a result, He's also taught me true humility, obedience, and courage. He knows my heart. There's nothing in my life that hasn't happened by His will. There's no place to go on this earth where He isn't. He is there, ready to be with you... ready to accept you, no matter where you've hidden, no matter what you've hidden from. He is there.

You see, Lord..............I haven't forgotten your words to this fallen child, from all those years ago. My prayer to you now is a simple one:

If not I Lord, then who? If not now Lord, then when? Amen.
- Your grateful son,

Todd Painton

VI

The Loner

Mike T.

Bad Luck's Victim

Eleven years of my life. Gone.

A few wrong turns in life and I was left isolated from the world. The pain and anger that coursed through my veins was enough to fill a couple of stadiums. I'd hit a brick wall of frustration. You see; it's not that I didn't know something was terribly wrong; it's just that I was unable to identify it. I couldn't and wouldn't reach out for help.

My distorted and miserable outlook on life had left me close to hopeless. My self-defeating attitudes and actions had led me to a point where I believed that death could be the only likely and somehow relieving option. On the surface I was alive...but on the inside, I was dead and would remain that way unless I could find a way to reach out for help. It felt like my will to live was slowly seeping out of me. I was depleted mentally, physically, and spiritually.

◆ ◆ ◆

As a child, I was well cared for and had the advantage of all the love my parents, grandparents, and other close relatives could shower on me. Everything considered, I had no real good reason to turn down a dark path later in life. I recall being a fairly happy child who played sports, had friends and a 'nothing could ever stop me' approach to life. I was always going to "have it all!"

At eight years old, I was a chunky, sarcastic kid with a highly developed mischievous streak. One day, looking out our bathroom window at my father washing the car in our driveway below, I thought it would be a cool trick to wad up some wet balls of toilet paper and throw them out the window on to the car so they would "mysteriously" splatter--resulting in pieces of paper littered across the fresh wash job. The next thing I remember is feeling the repeated sting of my dad's open hand across my flushed face. He proceeded to grab me by the ankles and hang me out the window to clean every trace of toilet paper off the garage roof shingles and then complete the recleaning of his precious car.

There was a distinct and hard-to-miss pattern developing: my sarcasm and defiance leading to my father going for 'the belt.' I would beg, plead and promise perfect behavior for the rest of my life...all to no avail. Once I realized the beating was unavoidable I would attempt to lessen the oncoming pain by stuffing magazines down my pant legs and behind my rear end...not that the effort did much good.

As a consequence of my actions at home and in school, I was also dutifully punished by filling entire yellow legal pads with "I will never" lists, swearing to never light fireworks off in school, never poke girls in the ass with pins, never be sarcastic to my mother again, never bring copies of Playboy to school again, etc. I'm sure the local office supply store was grateful for my personal contribution to their bottom line.

By the end of the sixth grade, Ms. McGlaughlin, my home-room teacher told me that she "expected a lot worse from me." That backhanded compliment allowed me to think that I was making some progress in my behavior. Seventh and eighth grade were manageable to the extent that no major catastrophes happened and I graduated. I was to then attend a Prep School where I really didn't know anybody. I felt as though I was sent there by my parents so they could tell friends their kid went to 'private school.' Little did I take into consideration that my parents lived pretty much paycheck to paycheck with no real purpose except to provide for their children and give us the best education and life.

My father's and my pattern of crime and punishment went beyond the context of our own household in my freshman year of high school. After hearing me mouth off to my mom, he beat the living sh-t out of me, giving me a black eye and a bloody nose. I remember him cleaning the blood out of the carpet, telling me the standard, 'it hurt him more than it hurt me.' The beating just happened to take place on a morning I was scheduled to take a school physical. Naturally, the doctor asked, "What happened to your eye?" I told him my father hit me, but that I deserved it. Sure enough, two days later we received a call from the city's child abuse agency. After a mild investigation they deemed it a one-time occurrence and no further action was recommended.

So there I was, a kid with an overdose of baby fat and not nearly enough self-esteem; attending a new school I didn't want to go to, with not a friend in the world. There were no good times anywhere near my horizon. To add to my nightmare, some smart-aleck bully decided to spread the bold-faced lie that he caught me masturbating in the gym shower. Of course the entire school started to treat me like a leper, and I had no idea why. When someone finally told me about the rumor, I was seething with anger.

I suppose most kids would have immediately ambushed the bully and at least attempted to knock him into another zip code, in defense of their reputation...but not me. The rage was there, and I dreamed of taking a baseball bat to this kid's face, beating it into ground chuck. I wanted to destroy him. But for whatever reason, when it came down to it, I just didn't know how to release my rage or pay the bastard back. I had rage and anger, but no outlet. I didn't do anything, and because I didn't, it devastated me.

Longing to fit in somewhere...anywhere, I gravitated to the "good-time" crowd that smoked a lot of weed during my sophomore year. I finally caught a social-acceptability break in my junior year and made the football team; but my true calling seemed to be drinking, smoking dope, and partying. This became my newfound identity. Whether or not I could wrangle an invitation to the "right" party became my obsession. And if I didn't get invited to that in-crowd party, the feelings of inferiority would overwhelm me. My self-esteem was always the first to take the hit...forcing me further and further into self-induced isolation.

Like most kids, I might have actually fit in, but I never really *felt* like I fit in. On one hand, I wanted to belong, but on the other, I was so uncomfortable that I began to see myself as the ultimate loner.

Aside from my family, I really didn't care about anyone in life (including myself), except for one man, my uncle. I was from a working-class family who never seemed to have much materially. But my uncle *had* made it in life. He worked hard as an accountant, and had all the things I wanted: a family, the beach house, social standing in the community. And on top of it all, he was a solid, honest man.

The more time I spent with him, the more I became comfortable with him. I felt as though he gave me purpose and blazed a trail of happiness that I wanted to follow. As a kid with a lot of uneasiness, he was the only person who put me at ease, taking me under his wing.

He trusted me and I trusted him, and I looked to him as a role model in all aspects of life. When it came to having dinner with my own family or with him, I chose him. My parents became understandably jealous, and I do have some remorse about that, but it was what it was. I developed a profound love for this man, who became my second father.

College arrived, and my uneasiness with my place in the universe gradually escalated. I partied like most students (so I thought). By scheduling all my classes late in the day, I had no problem drinking seven nights a week. In my junior year of college, I finally found a job that filled in all the blanks...bartending. The camaraderie of my patrons and co-workers was a high, and people loved me. For the first time, I started to feel comfortable in my own skin and just about that time I also found a major in school, Pharmaceutical Marketing, that I could relate to and actually looked forward to embracing.

So it looked like my anxieties were coming to an end. On a late summer Sunday in August, my uncle and I sat by the fireplace of his beach house overlooking the water. Without really saying a word, I had this overwhelming and undying sense of love for a man that treated me like his own and helped me as I was discovering a path that was finally beginning to take shape.

The very next day, my uncle was murdered.

An 80-year-old man whom my uncle had known for 25 years and provided business services to pro bono came over around 6 pm that Monday evening August 3rd, and wanted some of my uncle's time to discuss a business matter. My uncle was in the middle of an important project due the following day, and asked John if it could wait 'til tomorrow. Without warning and for no apparent reason, the 80-year-old pulled out a gun and fired three shots.

My uncle was heard telling him, "John, you hurt me once. Please don't hurt me again."

Two more shots were fired, and my uncle was dead. A senile old man had lost it and committed murder. There was no rhyme or reason.

The phone rang at my house that evening and as my mother answered the phone, she was heard yelling for my father, "Mike.. Mike..there's been an accident!!!" as she ran up the stairs. My father came down from the bedroom and the words came out, "Uncle Pat's been shot...Johnny shot Pat!" I have never seen or heard my father in such anguish as he yelled to the top of his lungs "Nooooooo!!" I pounded my fist on the kitchen counter, screaming "what the F---ck!!" and, in retrospect, I emotionally checked out right then and there.

I recall moaning, "I can't deal with this. I can't deal with this. I don't know how to deal with this!" The man who had given me so much had just been taken, never to return...I retreated back into isolation, my old comfort zone. And now, instead of reaching out for help, I chose to become isolated from the world to protect myself from the world. Not knowing what to do with my emotions, I suppressed them.

Four months later, still not having dealt with my uncle's passing, another friend was murdered and died in my arms.

It was one week before Christmas. I was tending bar, where we always clocked last call at 1:45 am. I had become friends with one of the regulars who had recently gotten married and was attending medical school around the corner. He had just finished his exams, and was celebrating—but now at 2 am he was pretty much in the bag.

A stranger came into the bar and asked for a drink. I told him, "Sorry we just had last call, can't serve you." He was annoyed and couldn't understand why he was not getting served. My friend, drunk, turned to him and said, "Do yourself a favor, beat it pal."

The stranger looked at my friend, nodded his head to the door implying, 'Let's take this outside.' But after no response, his gaze turns back to me and asked, "So you're not going to serve me?"

"Sorry, I can't."

To which he got up and walked out the door. Twenty minutes later my friend left, and two minutes after that, someone ran into the bar yelling my friend had been shot.

I'll never forget that cold and rainy December night. I ran across the street to the parking lot where a circle of people surrounded the scene. I found David still alive, and got on the ground, cradling him in my arms. "Hang on, buddy... hang on; help is on the way. Just hang on," I pleaded. But he died. I remember looking up into the dark sky, my face drenched, thinking, "What's it all for? What's life for if it can be snapped right out from under you?"

It was three days before Christmas. My uncle, the only man in life who gave me hope, had died...murdered. Now, a friend just died in my arms...murdered. Merry Christmas. I was emotionally dead. I didn't want to care for anything. Police station lineups, spending hours dealing with endless court proceedings, and testifying in the murder trial--occupied the bulk of my time. Meanwhile, I was still taking a full load at school, but trudging through life in a virtual fog.

Eleven months later, I sat down to study for an exam, and every page in the textbook was completely bare white. I turned each page, furiously searching for just one page to have any writing or a picture, but every page was blank...just like me inside. I broke down--shivering, shaking, convulsing, and crying. I pictured myself screaming at the top of my lungs, putting a gun to my head, and ending it all. I finally managed to fall asleep, and hoped that the morning would bring a return to rational thinking. No such luck. Two days later, I went to my parents' house to do laundry, dropped the basket just inside the front door and broke down, sobbing.

My parents immediately took me for help, and I was diagnosed with a classic and severe case of depression. I began taking Zoloft, not really knowing what it was. But for me, it didn't help. My wounds were so deep that no prescription could heal them. I was shut down emotionally. God was gone...after all, how could He allow such things to happen. Another joyless Christmas was about to come and go with no hope in sight.

And then, another death...a cousin committed suicide, and I told my mom, "That's what I wanted to do to *my*self."

My mom stepped back in shock and asked, mystified, "That's what you wanted to do to yourself??"

"Mom, you don't understand...when you hit that bottom, there's no other way out."

But I was actually already killing myself...just gradually. Alcohol and cocaine were becoming the constant in my life. The constant buzz they induced was my solace. I had self-prescribed steroids with the rationalization that I needed them to improve my gym workouts. I also mistakenly assumed that they could build my self-esteem and impress people. What people actually perceived was my new, over-the-top, "don't f-ck with me" attitude. My wall of isolation was becoming insurmountable. Escape, in every possible form, was my delusional answer. Every time I drove past the airport, I visualized myself on a plane, bound for anywhere, just taking off.

Shortly after graduating college, I did just that; I took off for California and continued my strict regimen of drinking, drugging, and courting misery. But what I was looking for in California wasn't to be found. Same uneasiness. Same thoughts. The only thing that changed was the zip code. And, as my unique form of luck would have it, I learned that my old girlfriend died in a car accident. When would people stop dying on me?

I returned back home, picking up with the same hard-partying crew like I had never left. We were in full roar every weekend. It seemed that I couldn't avoid the vicious cycle of "strictly business" Monday through Friday and then proceeding to obliterate myself, starting promptly at 5 pm Friday and not stopping until the sun came up the following Monday morning. And, of course, I was routinely coming in late to work, extremely hung-over.

One Monday, I was driving to work late, around noon. Steve, one of my co-workers, pulled up at the stoplight next to my car, rolled down his window, and asked if I wanted to go to lunch that day. Over cheeseburgers, I told Steve how miserable I was, and how lost I felt. Steve told me that he'd been there, and knew what I was experiencing. Today, I know that Steve was in a recovery program and was reaching out to help me.

Steve became the catalyst, valiantly attempting to place a mirror in front of a blinded version of me. He introduced me to his recovery group, and as our friendship grew I became a regular at the recovery meetings. But my attendance didn't slow my alcohol and coke intake. I continued my vain attempts at getting straight for another five years. The physical and emotional abuse I was subjecting my body and mind to, was still less painful than coming to terms with my own emotions.

But I had seen multiple therapists and checked myself into a bunch of out-patient rehabs. Nothing worked. One of the therapists I came to know just put it to me, plain and simple, by asking, "Mike, do you want to live?" There it was. It didn't take me more than a couple of seconds to respond, "I don't know."

> I didn't know *how* to live.
> I didn't know how to be accountable.
> I didn't know how to have dreams.
> I didn't know how to have goals.
> I didn't know how to get past my pain
> I didn't know how to have a relationship with
   myself, let alone others.
> I didn't know how to stop my chemical   dependency.

After isolating myself for 11 years, I committed myself to attend meetings of recovery every day for 90 days, knowing that if I didn't, I'd end up logging useless hours in yet another out-patient rehab.

Here's where the rubber met the road. Now I was experiencing the pain of dealing with emotions I'd been avoiding my entire adult life – all without the "assistance" of alcohol or drugs. I hated my straight life. As the emotions surfaced from deep within, they felt like tainted barbed wire being ripped through my body, second by second. And I was confident the excruciating pain wouldn't stop anytime soon. As I learned, the process involves "feeling, dealing, and then healing." It's the "and then" part...that seems to go on forever.

I have come to know, believe, and depend upon the foundation of recovery: 'A spiritual solution.' The one thing that helped me suffer though the process, is the faith I've found in God. Because I wasn't just recovering from drugs, alcohol and a hopeless state of life...I was recovering from a deep sickness of the soul. God is the only one that had, and will ever, have the power to gently yet confidently put my soul back together.

Steve, my mentor and friend, began to replace my uncle in many respects. He was 15 years older than me, and like me, had overcome giant personal obstacles. I began to see my uncle's spirit in Steve, and six years after I first met him, I discovered his birthday was the same day my uncle was murdered. I'm sure now that it was no accident he was placed in my life for a reason.

My being able to walk and talk, hold down a job, and give every appearance of normalcy was only a one-dimensional, cheap impersonation of life. It's clear to me that, for all intents and purposes, I was dead. There's a ton of hard work that lies ahead of me and it will be dedicated to regaining my soul and finding life again. Steve opened the door and showed me the way, and for that I'll always be grateful. But it's the teachings of Jesus Christ that have taught me that I am *not* alone; that God is here, standing by me and giving me strength from within.

It's also true that all the good intentions in the world are useless without taking the action necessary to expedite them. Talk is cheap and having faith without the willingness to work diligently, every waking minute, can only lead to an exercise in futility. It's my responsibility to develop a relationship with God first and foremost. I have grown and hopefully will continue to grow beyond my old fears, and further into faith. I have come to understand that in order to be loved, we must make ourselves accessible. Isolation is not an option for a fulfilled life.

People often hear me say, "I've tried to get through life and figure it out on my own; and for me, it just doesn't work." I've gathered the strength to be humble and accept the helping hands that are offered in every area of life. I can't do it alone, and I don't want to do it alone.

In addition to participating in a program of recovery, every Friday I gather with other men in a Gospel Reflection group where I can reconnect. I feel comfortable enough there to share my pain that was once shameful, but has today become the touchstone of my spiritual growth. I now have faith and confidence that I will make it through any tough times waiting for me, because I know I'm loved and I'm not carrying the burden alone.

Praying is now part of my daily regimen, almost like push-ups to improve the soul's strength and endurance. I pray that I may be shown God's will. I recently invited a fellow I met from out of town to the recovery meeting and he was very appreciative - sort of a "pass it on" concept for belief instead of charity. I'm getting stronger. And the stronger I become in my life, the more I'll be able to help others. I am no longer a victim of circumstances. I believe in my heart the strongest solution to our inherently broken lives is not escape, but a strong belief in God.

I've learned, despite all the complexities of my past, life is actually very simple. There are only two sides to life. One side... moving *away from* God, and the other...moving *closer* to God.

I've chosen my side.

VII

The Questioner
Mike Mullin

Why Should I Believe?
My life changed forever on April 25th, 2009. I answered my
phone at 5 o'clock that morning and immediately found myself
living in the epicenter of every parent's worst possible nightmare.
Our phone's terminally abrasive ring-tone jolted me awake and the
caller ID announced, in its female monotone voice, "Out of area."
At the time, that was my wife's and my signal that my youngest son,
Matt, was calling from Hong Kong. Matt had landed a job with
a technology company, and had been living there for more than a
year. Even half-asleep I knew something wasn't right. 5am here, 5
pm in Hong Kong…why would Matt be calling at this time? He'd
never wake us for something trivial. It seems ironic now, that most
days, my wife and I lived for his calls.

We would kid each other over who would win the race to
pick up the receiver to talk to him first. I answered the phone
with some anxiety in my voice to discover the person on the other
end was Matt's best friend in Hong Kong, Dave Larkin. I'd never
spoken to Dave before, but knew Matt had done a lot with him
in Hong Kong and considered him a great friend. Barely able to
speak, Dave introduced himself and blurted out, "Mr. Mullin, I
don't even know how to begin to tell you this…I am so sorry to
have to tell you this…Matt died in Hong Kong today."

I'll never ever forget those words…that frozen moment.

By this time my wife Sheila was out of bed getting ready to
speak with Matt, but she could hear me struggling to understand

the words that just hung there. How was I going to tell her that our youngest son was dead? I remember trying to shake the cobwebs of sleep out of my head - hoping and praying this was a part of a bad dream. Pacing the room with the phone in my hand, fear in my face, and anguish in my voice; the phone felt like it weighed 1,000 pounds as I started to realize this nightmare was to be my new reality.

"Dave...Dave slow down," I said trying to understand him over the anxiousness and tears in his voice. My wife sensed this was about Matt, and it was bad news. I remember stammering, "its Matt...Dave Larkin is saying that Matt died today in Hong Kong!" Horrified and heartbroken we tried to get the details from Dave. We were able to get the facts that Matt dove off a boat, hit his head, knocking him unconscious, and drowned.

And then the phone went dead.

Frantically trying to redial back to Hong Kong, Sheila and I were a mess. Several minutes later, another of Matt's friends called to confirm Dave's message and fill us in on everything he knew about the accident.

I remember thinking, "How could this be?" My wife and I just spoke to Matt about 15 hours earlier. We talked for about 45 minutes about his job, new friends, weekend plans, and his travel plans for the summer. Now it hit me I would also have to tell his brother, Mark, that Matt was dead. Just five months earlier, Matt was the Best Man in his brother Mark's wedding. With Mark and Matt being so close in age, they were each other's best friend... extremely close. I called Mark's line and got his voice mail knowing that he was likely out running or on an early bike ride. Within an hour, I told him his brother had died, and started pacing on my back steps, waiting for him to pull in the driveway. All I could do while I looked for his car was cry.

And sooner than later, I was overtaken by a giant wave of anger.

Just a few months earlier, I had prayed to God to keep my son safe while he was in Hong Kong. And I recalled the line from the book of John in the Bible which said, "…and whatsoever ye shall ask in my name, that will I do, that the Father may be glorified in the Son."

It was during the Lenten season a few months earlier, my wife and I decided to each make a sacrifice that would be special, so I decided to participate in our church's round-the-clock adoration, where members of the congregation schedule their prayer times so that no hour is left uncovered. The hour I drew was 1 am-2 am—hardly the best time slot for a guy in the construction industry who had to get up early. I drew the first Thursday of each month during Lent, and I told my wife I was planning on spending that dedicated time asking God to keep Matt safe while far from home. In my first hour of devoted prayer, I felt my relationship with God leap to a whole new level. I remember feeling closer to God than ever before in my life and I was confident that He would grant my simple, yet specific, request to keep Matt safe. I had faith.

But now my son was gone! What happened to that line from John 14? I trusted you God, but you let me down! Yes accidents happen, but eerily enough, I must have somehow sensed Matt would need extra prayers - extra protection. And now this! Did you lie to me God? If not, are you sending me some kind of life message? How am I supposed to trust in you now? Speak to me! The questions never stopped, and the answers never came.

◆　◆　◆

For 15 years, every morning on my commute to work, I had passed a local cemetery which had a large white cross on the top of a hill. It was easily seen from the road and every single day I'd look up from the wheel and silently pray at the sight of this simple but classic symbol of my faith. Thousands of times throughout the years I'd blessed myself and asked Him for special intentions, inspired by the sight of this cross.

So how could this happen? Why…why now? Why my son? What did he do to deserve this? Why should my wife and family be permanently saddened? What did *they* do to deserve this? I felt like God had kicked me in the teeth. I was numb. My faith in Him was washed away. My relationship with Him was hopelessly broken.

Deadened with our sadness, we met with our church pastor before the 7.30 mass that Sunday morning, told him the particulars about Matt's passing, and asked him to bless our journey to Hong Kong later that day. We asked the pastor and congregation to pray for two things. First, that the Hong Kong Marine recovery team would somehow be able to find Matt's body. And second, that we would be able to bring Matt home for a proper burial. I still clearly remember my rage and hopelessness at asking for these things when I really didn't have any belief that He was there to listen or care. I guess I still believed in the power of prayer...just not the power of *my* prayer. We received the news just before boarding the plane, that after 15 hours of uncompromising effort by the Hong Kong Marine Police in those dark waters, Matt's body had been found. I recognized God's mercy, as we were going to Hong Kong to bring Matt home. Were those my prayers that were answered, or others on our behalf?

The four of us (my wife and I, my son Mark, and his new bride) booked the first available non-stop flight to Hong Kong. The long flight seemed completely cloaked in silence and Dave greeted us at the gate with more grief on his face than I'd ever witnessed on a young man. Matt's closest friends were waiting for us at the hotel to offer awkward condolences and many loving stories of their departed friend. Then, we drove to the small remote town of Sai Kung, 45 minutes outside of Hong Kong. Our destination was the public mortuary where the authorities had brought our son.

I'll never forget that first morning in Hong Kong: the building, the red tape, the people, the cab ride and all the details leading up to the point when the gurney holding Matt was wheeled out into the waiting area. The dream-like haze that enveloped us since the phone call, came to an abrupt end when we saw our Matt's cold body for the first time. We were crushed and heartsick as we reached out for him. He had a severe injury over his left eye that was probably the result of where he hit the boat and was knocked unconscious into the water. We helplessly caressed his face and head. The Chinese attendant was indifferent to our tears, showing no reaction at all to our sorrow and devastation. He commenced rattling off the standard government procedure, which would include the performance of a full autopsy. I immediately objected, but soon realized that we'd have to navigate an unfamiliar foreign legal system to prevent my son from being cut open. A wonderful woman from Matt's office helped us contact the right people, visit the correct offices, fill out the required forms, and get our appeal finally granted. Without this and the 'Death of an American Citizen Abroad Certificate', there would be no way to take the body back to the U.S. We were dealing with the many, newly enforced Homeland Security protocols that had been put in place post 9/11. During the middle of week, more than a hundred of Matt's friends and co-workers organized a memorial service. We were bowled over by their generosity and outpouring of love.

◆ ◆ ◆

In retrospect, the loss I was feeling that day, and still feel to this day, goes far beyond my son's physical absence. Matt's death caused me to doubt every single thing I ever held to be true. We are all taught, our whole lives, if you work hard you will be rewarded for your efforts. I had always put stock in the theory that if you give of yourself, you will be rewarded with long and lasting relationships. I had truly believed that if you strive to do the right thing in life, life will be good to you. Or, so I thought.

Matt had it all. His engaging and multi-faceted personality allowed him to be a wonderful son, a loving brother, a dedicated and loyal friend, and a trusted associate. He was handsome, with a well-sculptured frame that women stopped to notice. He had a ridiculous work ethic, achieving and succeeding in everything he attempted. His laid-back easy style with family and friends was only slightly unsettled by his intense drive; he wanted to be two or three places at the same time to accomplish his goals. He was easy to get to know, and enjoyed new people and experiences.

At the funeral, one of his pals said, "Nobody knew the balance between hard work and play better than Matt." From the time he was in grade school, I knew I wouldn't have to worry about him succeeding. He was a go-getter, who got it early. He knew hard work, he knew people, and he knew the power of giving...not just taking. He loved his family and friends. He loved life, knowing there was only 24 hours in a day, always trying to get the most out of every day. He had an infectious sense of humor. He was caring and compassionate. When you were with him, he made you feel like you were the most important person in the room.

And perhaps he was a better man than I. The last day, the last time, I was with him--it was the Sunday after Thanksgiving, the most traveled day of the year, two days after being the Best Man in his brother's wedding. He had a flight back to Hong Kong leaving at 3pm. He stayed with friends the previous night to take advantage of every minute he could spend with them. Inevitably, we left for the airport later than planned. I was more than slightly stressed out; knowing that it was the Sunday after Thanksgiving and traffic would be terrible. Knowing we were late and that we'd most likely hit lots of traffic, I started to bitch, which started the two-hour drive to the airport on a stressful note. The traffic was horrendous, and after numerous back-and-forth jabs at each other throughout the drive, a thought came over me that, "God forbid, what if this was the last time we were together? What if, God forbid, this would be the last time I saw him?" I immediately settled in to a better mindset, shut off my worried venting, and finally began to enjoy each other's company the rest of the ride to the terminal. He hopped out when we arrived, and five minutes later was back with news that the airline wouldn't let him check in because he was 10 minutes late. So he missed his flight that day... the next one didn't leave until tomorrow.

Here was the difference in our reactions. I was pissed at him. How was he going to explain missing his flight to his boss? Am I going to have to drive him home and do this all over again the next day, and have to take a vacation day? But Matt, just smiled and said, "It's OK Dad. Drive me to Hoboken. I'll get to spend another night with Tommy." That was Matt – changing a negative to a positive as easily as changing lanes on a midnight freeway. He taught me a real lesson. Maybe I should take it as a compliment that I was able to raise a better man than I could ever be. I dropped Matt at Tommy's never thinking it would be the last time I'd see my son alive. I stood behind the car outside his apartment, hugged him, telling him I loved him. The last thing I said was "Matty, be well. Come home safe... Love ya, pal."

The reality is that there is no way to make this better. No way to change the circumstances of my son's accident. No way to change the circumstances that ended his life. No way to heal the broken hearts of his mother and brother. No way to mend the hurt of his close friends. No way to ever feel the love he showered on us every day of his life.

It is What it Is.

We heard this phrase again and again while dealing with the Chinese authorities. The concept of "It is what it is," was as ambiguous and foreign to me as China itself.

Growing up in an Irish Catholic family of nine, my hard-working mother and father always used the phrase, "Where there's a will, there is a way." The spirit they instilled in me by their example and hard-driving work ethic was now standing in the way of accepting a new brand of reality. We always believed if we worked hard enough we could overcome any adversity. We would find a way to conquer any problem that challenged us—with will. We believed in the awesome power of prayer and that God was there to answer our prayers. "If we knocked" as it says in the book of Matthew, He would be there for us.

So where was my God now? I thought the kind of tragedy I was experiencing only happened to other people. Not me. I was grieving, and the pain was deep within me. My eyes were sore, my body lacked energy, and it didn't diminish, even after 17 months. Why did this have to happen? I'm still angry that my son didn't get a second chance. Thousands of absurd scenarios keep swirling around in my head. Why was he knocked unconscious when he hit his head instead of maybe just cut, allowing him to call for help? Why couldn't his friends Dave, Sam, or Aidan, who were in the gray water within seconds looking for him, find and rescue him before he drowned? They were only feet, perhaps just inches, from his body in the water. They will always be affected by the memory of their failed attempt. Why leave them with a feeling of not knowing how close they could have been to saving him? Questions attack my mind; some logical and others, completely based in fantasy, day after day. Any coherent answers have always eluded me.

Where to From Here?

Years earlier while attending church services, I would sit in the pew and occasionally observe a man or a woman who had lost a son or daughter through accident or illness and comment to my wife on the way home how horribly sad they must be. I watched them and saw their incompleteness. I would say to my wife they must have a missing piece somewhere--a void that will never be filled. Now, I am one of their brothers and I hate it.

I'm concerned about how my wife will handle her broken heart. I'm anxious about how to keep Matt from becoming the main topic of every conversation with my son Mark. Before the accident, I was going to Church most every Sunday, but I wasn't 'all in.' I was just checking the boxes as they say. I'd say that if my faith was measured on a scale of 1 to 10, I would fall a little right of center, about a 6. After the accident, I gradually slipped to a low of a 3, attending Mass but not really feeling comfortable being in His house. During Mass I was unable to look to God for support or pray for the grace I so desperately needed to get through another day. I used to be a guy who, when I woke in the morning at 5 am, was shot out bed like a cannon to take the day by storm. My mornings had changed from being fully charged with energy...to a sad march of habitual motion. I was hitting the sack earlier and earlier, to simply to get the day over with. I had little motivation to start the next day knowing Matt wasn't going to be there.

Shortly after the accident, I found myself wishing that I could roll the calendar ahead one full year, thinking that would allow me to be a year into the grief…with some amount of emotional healing already taken place. After a year and a few months, the pain was still kicking my ass: physically, mentally, emotionally, and spiritually.

With Nowhere to Turn, I Turned Back to Him.

They say that the root of pure faith is trust. I trusted God to keep my son safe, but the Bible also says that Jesus is the way, the truth, and the life. I hate the cards I've been dealt, but I'm now going to believe (and trust) that Jesus is the way, the truth, and the life. Even after my prayers were not answered for whatever reason…I now have to trust that He knows the reasons and wrap my mind around accepting that I may never know those reasons, perhaps until I'm reunited in heaven with my son. I don't know if my faith is fully restored, but I trust that I can heal as this existence continues…and continue my journey. Because I know God wants me to, and as much as it hurts…I have faith that my son Matt also wants me to.

I believe God will give me the grace of spirit to compensate for this most-precious missing piece of my life. One step forward, one day at a time. I'll keep moving on the journey, even though I'm hurt, dazed, and often confused.

Maybe Now

I think it's important to note that with this tragedy, some wonderful new people have come into our lives, while others, important in our lives before the accident, have remained distant. These people, I'm guessing, simply don't know what to say or do to comfort us. There is an awkwardness that seems to paralyze normally kind and caring people surrounding Matt's death and our grief. Matt's close friends from home and Hong Kong have been and continue to be unbelievably kind and supportive, never forgetting, always checking in to say Hi with concern about our healing. We treasure our new friendship with them. Another new person is a special man, Euse Mita, and I'm sure it was no accident that I bumped into him after Mass one day. He extended an open invitation to me to join him anytime on Friday morning for a Gospel Reflection group he organized. I didn't take advantage of the opportunity at that time but it did plant the seed to something that might help. I told him I might attend some time in the future. Well the future was a few months later when I ran into another friend, Eddy, who I hadn't seen in years and invited me to a attend the same Friday morning gospel reflection group. I was a little hesitant because I wasn't much of a scripture reader on my own, and had a vision of guys sitting around reading the gospel, getting over-wrought, excited, and holier-than-thou. As distant from my faith as I had become, it occurred to me that maybe these meetings could help me find a way back to my belief system. I called Eddy, and with some trepidation, arranged to go to my first meeting. I had no idea what I would find.

As it turns out, the group of open, trusting, and caring men I have come to know and appreciate have made all the difference in my finding and recreating an ongoing relationship with the Lord. I was able to get to know other men in the group who had experienced more than their fair share of trouble, sadness, and tragedy and they were not afraid to offer their stories, their comfort, and their support to me. Through this group and the gospel reflection they share, I have come to believe that the Lord does understand my loss, and through his grace I will experience the love of His mercy. I am not whole, and perhaps no man is, but I am beginning to understand again that He is present in my life and will guide me through this sadness with His everlasting love for me. I believe that I will be reunited with my son again someday and the answers to the questions will be revealed to me. And I believe that in order for that miracle to take place I need to step up my faith, my actions, and my trust in Him. I believe that I need to now look for his will in everything I do. I start and end my day with Him and ask that I be mindful of His presence in my life and also look for my son's presence as I go about my journey of healing. I believe there is no going back to what was. I'm a different person now, a changed disciple, a follower who believes in the healing power of the Holy Spirit.

Rev, David Sauter S.J. made the following offering at Matt's funeral Mass:

"What does the Lord ask of you, my son? Only this: to act

justly, to love tenderly, and to walk humbly with your God. Matt was kind and just to every one he met, he loved each of us for who we were and not for the person he, or even we, wanted us to be, and he knew that the gifts God had given him were not to be taken for granted and kept to himself alone, but they were to be developed and used for the good of others. Our hearts are heavy, but we rejoice that we were among those privileged to have known and loved Matt. We miss Matt deeply, but how blessed we were to have had him in our lives. God weeps with us and feels our pain. But if Matt brought God to us while he walked among us, how much more will he do it now that he is with God in person. Let us pray today in the depths of our mourning that we might follow his example and act justly, love tenderly, and walk humbly with our God".

I am now committed to my Lord, to Matt, to my loving wife Sheila, to my extraordinary son Mark and also to my Friday morning group of good friends.

I still pass that big white cross on the highway, on my way to and from work. And I still pause, bless myself but say, "Jesus, I now place all my trust in You." The football field we have to play on in this earth, is a valley of tears; and on this field we have to learn to play hurt. And although I may not like playing hurt, it is what it is. There is nowhere else to turn, nowhere else to go, but back to Him.

Mike Mullin

V III

The Rebel
Bill LaMorey

Rage Against the Machine

"To rebel ...." to resist or rise against some authority, control, or tradition."

Many stories have been told of noble rebels - famous men and women throughout history, who valiantly and sacrificially rebelled against unjust and unfair systems to stand up for the people marginalized by them. Abraham Lincoln, Susan B. Anthony and Martin Luther King Jr. immediately come to mind as notable examples of people whose courage and imagination led to confrontation, which eventually resulted in constructive change for society. However, this was not the definition of "rebel" that fits the man I became.

My version lacked any reason, purpose, or nobility. In addition to being difficult, the rebel's highway I chose was painful, destructive, and nearly succeeded in killing me before turning twenty-five.

What makes a rebel? Is it genetics, environment, culture, or is it good old Rock & Roll? Consider the straightforward simplicity of this statement:

"There are those who rebel against the light; they do not know its ways nor abide in its paths." (Job 24:13)

It's interesting that this verse from the Bible doesn't say why some people rebel. It just says, "There are those" who do. I've often wondered about my own propensity to resist authority, and to generally "rage against the machine." Was it because my father died when I was five years old? Was it because my stepfather, who lived with us for five years, was an alcoholic and physically abused my mother? Was it because I had very little discipline in my formative years? Maybe these things did contribute to the path I took. And maybe they were just convenient excuses for my out-of-control behavior. I don't know. What I can be sure of is that I did rebel against the light, and that my chosen path led me into some very dark and undesirable places.

Trying to kill my babysitter at age four would qualify, at the very least, as a rebellious act. All I can remember is that I didn't appreciate whatever the babysitter was telling me to do and how she was telling me to do it. So, when she asked me to get her a glass of water one day, I saw my big chance for mutiny. I poured her water and then went upstairs and dumped in every cleaning product, medicine, soap and vile thing I could find, into the same glass. Toddler logic convinced me that once the babysitter drank my potion, my problems would all be over! My fantasies of how I would spend my newfound freedom were interrupted when she asked if I had done anything to her water. "No," I lied as the toxic brew in her hands fizzled and bubbled. Some might dismiss this as mere childish behavior, but it set the tone and pace for a recurring life theme.

School was always problematic for me. No one would ever be able to accurately guess my actual IQ after hearing some of the incredibly stupid stunts I pulled. My mom had sacrificed financially to send me to a private Christian middle school where I quickly became their problem project. I was regularly sent to the principal's office for class clown behavior and general disregard for authority. After several visits to the principal, which all resulted in fairly severe paddling, I decided to leave rather than "take it like a man." After these unannounced sabbaticals, I was told I could either accept an "early graduation" from the 8th grade or be expelled. I was thrilled with my unexpected graduation.

The label 'criminal' would be a stretch, but I got involved with more than my share of criminal mischief. At nine, I became friends with Freddy, whom I later dubbed my "criminal mentor."

Freddy taught me how to shoplift, and how to pawn items for cash. It was his idea to patrol the downtown shopping districts wearing school basketball uniforms, supposedly collecting money for a team charity. Of course, the day's take would go straight into our pockets. All this was done for thrills and walking-around money. Our delinquent partnership was officially dissolved when we got busted for breaking & entering. The police caught us, and the prosecutor made it a point to arrange a "let's scare the kid to death" meeting with me alone in a closed-door session. He agreed not to press charges after giving me a crystal-clear picture of what could happen if I ever got caught again.

Once home, my stepfather decided it would be an excellent time for me to know the truth about my real father. He told me my real father had not died in a car crash as I had always been told; but had been shot and killed while robbing a liquor store. I couldn't believe it. I felt deeply hurt, confused and angry as the truth of my father suddenly got harder to bear as it went from tragic to sinister. My stepfather chose this moment to divulge the secret, hoping it would scare me straight. For a while it worked, but as time went on, it just made me hate him even more.

By eleven, my mother and stepfather were separated. Shortly after the split-up she found Jesus. Initially, I went for the JC deal too and regularly attended church with Mom for a few years. My attendance dwindled to occasional and holiday services. Finally, one particular Christmas service confirmed all the negative notions I'd ever had about church. I now had what I thought was the justification to hate it with a passion. As I sat in the pew with my rock-star long hair, one woman behind me "whispered" to another, "He only comes on Christmas and Easter!" Not skipping a beat, I turned around, looked her in the eye and said, "And that's my business isn't it?" The woman's mouth dropped in horror and she stopped her whispering. I was angry, slightly amused, but mostly really angry. That episode became my long-time memory of why I didn't like church and why I never had much use for churchgoers. So I stopped going.

My path of rebellion continued and led me to places and habits

I vowed to avoid. Having seen the ravaging effects of drug and alcohol abuse on my family, I swore off these vices in my own life.

But at nine, I was drinking. And at thirteen, I was smoking pot. At fourteen, I was dropping acid. At fifteen, I was at a David Lee Roth concert and after power-drinking shots of Jack Daniels like lemonade shooters, I blacked out in the stadium bathroom. Waking up in the emergency room with fluorescent lights above, a nurse informed me I just had my stomach pumped, and nearly died of alcohol poisoning. The nurse continued her stern lecture, telling me that if I'd thrown back even one more shot of JD, I would have died. Then I looked over and saw my mother standing by the bed, sad and disappointed. At that moment, I almost wished I had died. For a couple years I kept away from the bottle, but I found more creative outlets for my self-absorbed rebellion.

At seventeen, I met the infamous 90's rock star, Marilyn Manson at a Ramones concert in South Beach. He was handing out flyers for his very first show. We spent some time hanging out and became friends. I was a regular at all the Marilyn Manson shows and got the chance to conduct and write an interview on him for a local music publication. Eventually I was dubbed Marilyn's "Minister of Information", because of my unique ability to stir up perceived controversy and exaggerated drama to hype the band. My efforts just added fuel to the national media fire concerning the blasphemy of Marilyn's satanic stage antics.

We thrived on the dark humor and the cartoon-like imagery of any satanic visual we discovered; we thought it was all a big joke. So much so that Marilyn or Brian (Manson's real name is Brian Warner) and I would shop every Christian bookstore in Fort Lauderdale, looking for plastic Jesus action figures to convert into Charles Manson dolls. One afternoon, walking out of one store with our freshly purchased treasure, a customer asked, "Are ya'll in a band or somethin'?" Brian choked back his laughter while I quickly went into a whole bit about how we were an up-and-coming Christian rock band called "Satan on Fire" and urged him to check out our next performance, which was actually the next Manson show. From that day on, "Satan on Fire" became the phony Christian band for which I created and distributed fake flyers, actually steering a completely straight-laced demographic to Manson's semi-disturbing shows.

So there I was, taking the image of Jesus Christ, converting it into a Charles Manson image, and duping Christians into coming to Satan-friendly rock concerts. For someone who no longer believed in God or the devil, I sure was working hard against the former for the latter. When you think of a rebel, you usually think of someone with more than their fair share of hidden rage. I guess I was angry enough, but I was really just sad…deeply sad. Hope was not in my vocabulary. Of course, I never showed that side of me. The side of me everyone got to see was the non-stop Court Jester. My laugh was the mask I used to cover my pain. The prideful, obnoxious, humorous, rebellious rocker and prankster was a scared boy who was lost, hurt, and confused – a prime candidate for alcohol and drug abuse.

I started with prescription opiates. By twenty-one, I was on heroin. Most kids looked forward to buying booze at twenty-one…me, heroin. It made my depression and pain vanish. In my extensive research to find the ultimate high, I discovered the "speedball," a syringe-injected cocktail of heroin and cocaine. And that led me to the lowest and darkest place in my life: a full-blown heroin addict.

Most heroin addicts end up dead or in detox. I landed in detox. As I dealt with the worst-ever imaginable flu-like symptoms of withdrawal multiplied by 50, I looked down at my feet and stared at the smiley faces on the foam slippers that came standard issue with every bed. Those smiley faces made me furious! I remember thinking they might as well have been middle fingers directed up at me, because there was very little in my life to smile about. The countless sleepless nights of sweating, vomiting, and writhing in more than the worst pain you can envision crept by like molasses. Seconds seemed to be minutes. Minutes felt like hours. All in screaming pain. My body pitifully begged for heroin, my only solace.

You'd think that given my position, I would've given in to the process of getting clean. However, my rebellious instincts were so engrained, I fought the recovery process itself. A mandatory piece was attending a 12-step program. I was already aware of the basically God-centered process that had helped millions of people, but I already made up my mind that it couldn't work for me. I was too smart for my own good. My argument was that if I had a so-called "disease", then prescribing a moral cure over a medical one was ludicrous. Turning control of my life over to the still-foreign concept of "God" seemed equally impossible to digest.

I was sure that if there was a God, I should find out EXACTLY who He is and then worship Him on His terms. But, I wasn't quite ready to give church another shot. So I stopped attending the 12-step meetings and quickly drifted back to my dangerous, yet somehow comfortable, junkie status.

I was challenging life and courting death with reckless abandon. In retrospect, something or someone must have been working double-overtime to keep me alive. I arrived in a local ER one night with blood streaming out of my mouth - just coherent enough to fear I'd overdosed from a lethal cocaine injection, but so high I didn't realize I'd taken a bite out of my tongue. Another night, in an opiate stupor, I almost injected a full syringe of bleach into my veins, which could have easily been my last attempt at escape. My depression hit me so hard that spring, I purposely copped enough smack to end my life permanently. Luckily, I was so stoned that when I finally gathered my nerve to do the deed, I couldn't find the stash that would end it all. Amazing; knowing that junkies keep track of their stash more diligently than most stockbrokers keep track of their shares. I don't remember ever losing drugs before, but after the fog lifted, I was certainly glad that I had. Sure, my self-destructive episodes scared me...but not enough to wake me up.

I remember another incident where a girl and I had scored some super high-grade heroin. As soon as she tied herself off and shot up, I knew that she was in serious trouble. Seconds after the needle punctured her skin, she fell to the floor, her face turned blue, and instantly lost consciousness. After racing to hide the remaining drugs, I called 911 and proceeded to wait in a blind panic. I wasn't sure if she was going to live or die, and if I would spend the rest of my life behind bars for manslaughter. When the paramedics came, they were able to save her life by injecting her with Narcan. The police searched my house, and promptly arrested me for felony possession.

Enduring the excruciating pains of withdrawal and dreading the outcome of the upcoming sentencing, I called my mom from jail. I pleaded with her to bail me out. Her first reaction was to refuse. She let me cool my heels in jail for a couple of days, and only got me out after I agreed to enter a Christian addiction program called Calvary House. As usual, my plan was to lay low at Calvary House, ride out the legal storm, and get back to getting high as quickly as possible. Continuing my pattern of rebellion, I got myself kicked out of Calvary House three different times. After each ejection, I found my way straight back to Heroin Central. On my last junkie bender (which lasted about a year) I swore I'd never return.

Supporting my habit usually entailed working, then selling everything I owned, and when I ran out of stuff, I would steal anything that wasn't tied down. What's worse is that my victims were my close friends and family. I would rip them off (stealing just about anything) and turn around and sell it on the street–the typical MO of any hopeless addict. One of these unsuspecting victims was my roommate. Her boyfriend and I were drug buddies and she nailed us after we sold hundreds of her CDs over a couple of months. When she confronted us she said we had to get professional help immediately, or she'd call the police and turn us in. I was in violation of my probation, so I was at least coherent enough to understand that another stay at Calvary House wasn't my best choice; it was my only choice.

This time, my plan was to stay in rehab just long enough to appease my former roommate, while accumulating enough money to go on yet another colossal binge! (sound familiar?) I thought that I was "the man with the plan." What I didn't expect, however, was that the "light" that I'd rebelled against my entire life was about to shine through the wall I'd so carefully built – and do so with undeniable intensity, illuminating a path of hope and healing. That's what I'd always needed and wanted, but thought I was too far gone.

Back at Calvary House, I was daily and forcefully encouraged to place my faith in Jesus. But the headstrong rebel in me still resisted submitting to God's authority. As part of the routine there, men in the program worked on the facility's property during the day and then attended Bible studies or church services at night. The entire Calvary House crew, my mom and her friends, and a bunch of other people would watch me intently, as Pastor Bob Coy's service would proceed. They all wondered if that night would be the night I would walk forward in response to the altar call, and surrender my life to Jesus. I left them wondering for months, but God was patiently working on me. Finally, during a service, I came to believe that Jesus was really God. And maybe, just maybe, He might be able to help me. So I decided to take a chance with Jesus, and made the slow stroll down the long aisle amidst a thunderous roar of those who had watched me stubbornly resist for months.

I prayed for Jesus to enter my heart, but a prayer is only the first small step. You don't go from punk to perfect on the wings of a simple prayer. But the process began and I applied myself to praying and reading my Bible regularly while my internal battle still raged within me. Part of me wanted to walk down God's path. But part of me wanted to retain control of my life and return to the place where I was free to destroy myself.

One of my challenges was that I really wanted to embrace change, but part of me still felt dirty, tainted, and untouchable... like I didn't belong in church with these polished, pretty people. I watched a gorgeous blonde with a beautiful smile seemingly float into church one day, and I imagined what it might be like to be in a relationship with a clean, wholesome girl like her. But, even fantasizing about a real relationship with a 'normal' girl seemed delusional to me. I often felt the same way about the chances of starting any kind of relationship with God.

But the afternoon of March 15, something broke loose. Calvary House was located in the middle of a rough, drug-infested neighborhood, and I watched the regular strolling pack of prostitutes and drug dealers hustling their wares on the corner. As I watched one drug deal go down, I wondered, "God, am I just fooling myself here? Or is it just a matter of time before I'm lined up behind that guy paying good money to destroy myself again?"

Right at that moment, I felt a sense of peace – a sense that eluded me for years. The dark clouds of the afternoon shifted and sunlight pushed through the room against my face...warming my entire being. It was as if God let me feel His presence and reassured me that I was going to be OK. It felt as if He was telling me that this chapter of my life was coming to an end. The phrase I heard God say was from Ecclesiastes. I heard Him say, "It's time to heal."

This was my "now" moment. I got it. I had a long distance to go, but from that point on, I knew I was ready for a new chapter to begin. I had no idea what would happen, but I was determined to spend the rest of my life journeying on the path I had resisted my entire life...God's path.

Untangling the mess I had made of my life was going to be rough. Although I had come to terms with the fact there was a ton of work ahead, I really had no idea how to deal with my upcoming sentencing for my third probation violation. I was pretty scared. There was a good chance I'd have to serve up to a year in prison. I knew that I would never achieve peace until I dealt with all of the unresolved issues and the outstanding debts racked up in my sordid past. I'd just have to put aside my fear.

So, I surrendered myself to the court. Paul Whetstone, the original Director of Calvary House, and I entered the courthouse together on the appointed day and I was determined to accept whatever my fate would be. As I stood in front of the all-too familiar judge, and explained where I had been and where I was now, the Judge stared at me for what seemed like an eternity and said, "Son, you are a different person...I can see you've found God. I can see it in your eyes." I prayed for a long time the night before, but I didn't have the nerve to pray for what happened next. To the strong objections of the prosecutor, the judge decided that I would serve no prison time, and waived probation. He gave me a clean slate in the criminal justice system. If you're familiar with the three-strikes-and-you're-out probation rule, you know that this could never happen...only in a miracle.

I knew God was on my side, working to provide every opportunity to succeed in my new adventure with Him. It was now up to me to make good choices with God's guidance. One of the best choices I made was to remain a part of the church I attended even after I left Calvary House. Though I was insecure, I came to realize that nobody in the crowd was perfect, and nobody had it all altogether. They were *just* as messed up as I was. Everyone there was a work in progress, growing with God's help and grace just like I was. I couldn't believe I'd gone from dreading church twice a year to loving it twice a week.

The prospects of gainful employment for people with a criminal record and no college degree aren't rosy, so job-hunting was going to be an uphill battle for me. I wanted to cover up my past, but I had to let God lead. I decided to take the risky approach of sharing my story upfront, instead of letting a potential employer discover my dirt in the interview. One guy named Bob Levin, the owner of a small business called Clay, Metal & Stone, took a chance on me despite my past and offered me a job. With a generous opportunity from Bob and the plentiful flow of God's grace, I excelled in the 4 &1/2 years I worked there.

I thought of going back to school. Years earlier, before my addiction escalated, I was able to keep a 4.0 GPA in honors classes at community college.

Ultimately, I felt that I was being guided to attend Bible College. I was sure this would slow down other aspirations; but it felt right, so I registered. As if by plan (certainly not my plan), my business trek seemed to prosper while I pursued an education in Theology. Go figure. Clay, Metal & Stone first hired me to start as a Customer Service rep, but I was promoted to General Manager in record time with no college degree or formal business training. God had me on the fast track.

As I got serious about pursuing God and His path, it became necessary to sever most of my old friendships. This was very difficult and painful because I genuinely cared about my friends, but it was necessary because most of the relationships were mutually toxic. Although the right thing to do, it left me incredibly lonely. I learned how to have fun in good and healthy ways. I discovered you could have a good time eating wings, drinking Coke, and watching the Florida Panthers. I was able to meet a whole new crew of friends who kept me focused, accountable and encouraged as I pressed forward with God. These guys were essential.

But as I watched all my friends get engaged and get married, I still felt like damaged goods. Shame dominated my feelings of self-worth, and insecurity ran rampant when I looked in the mirror every morning. Because of my past, I was convinced that the only girl who would even consider being with me would be someone with as much baggage and history as I had. But remember the beautiful blonde with the great smile? I got to know her a little at some church functions and it turns out her past was *exactly* like her image. She was a goody two-shoes cheerleader in high school who never touched drugs or associated with junkies. *She* actually said yes when I asked her out! We dated, and she's now my wife, best friend, and the fantastic mother of our three beautiful daughters. She is the single biggest testimony to God's grace in my life.

In the last few years, I've been able to see the result of God's work. He didn't just redesign and reconstruct pockets of my life like work, school, friends and family. God actually gave me the chance to redeem my entire rebellion allowing me the opportunity to reach for the reason, and purpose, I'd been missing all those years. With God, everything changed. God led me out of the dark places of my past and then, when I was strong enough, made it possible for me to go right back to the exact locations of my many falls from grace; this time as a keeper of the flame...now able to lend a hand to others trying to find their footing.

Calvary House, with its once sterling reputation as a beacon in the recovery movement, had fallen on hard times and was now in a state of total disrepair. Its once highly disciplined ministry had become a mere shadow of its former self - a flophouse with some Bible studies thrown in as an afterthought. Paul Whetstone, the founder and original director, was gone. His replacement's wife had run off with an addict in the program. The next Director returned to the needle himself, and died of a heroin overdose. The church was on the brink of closing down the program that was responsible for saving my life. But through an amazing set of circumstances I was chosen to return and lead Calvary House five years after I graduated the program. Truly...the inmates were now running the asylum. We were given one year to turn it around. With God's grace, we did it and Calvary House thrives to this day healing addicts like the one I once was.

Three years later my business experience, my biblical education, and a slight push from God made me a perfect fit for my next opportunity. I was asked to join my Bible College friend Bob Franquiz as his church's Administrative Pastor. The church was in the same North Miami district where most of my former pharmaceutical distributors (drug dealers) had operated. For a long time I had made it my business to avoid this area, and now God helicopter-dropped me right back in the thick of it. Now, I came to realize that this wasn't the finish line, but just the starting line.

Most of my family is originally from Connecticut and I went back every once in a while to visit. Every time I was there, I got bugged by the severe lack of thriving churches. It was a shocking contrast to South Florida, where in town after town, vibrant churches abound. New England was once the epicenter of spiritual activity. But now, 400 years later, Connecticut is one of the least religious states in the U.S. ...ranked in the bottom five. Connecticut's overt need for a spiritual renaissance gradually became a burning passion for me. So I prayed for someone to go and start a church there. Through a series of signals, God made it clear that I should stop praying and become that very person. Roll the calendar forward five years... now I'm the Pastor of Calvary Fellowship (West Hartford, CT). We began with me, my wife and first daughter, and the church has grown from nothing to well over 200 people in average weekly attendance. I used to hate going to church and now I lead one as its pastor. Who says God doesn't have a sense of humor?

God used my past to make me a better person, and now gives me the privilege of helping make circumstances around me better. That's how God works. He redeems broken people and then uses them to redeem what's broken around them.

While I was a 'client' at Calvary House someone told me if I follow God, He would do more than I could ever ask, think, or imagine. He would accept me, as imperfect as I am. I scoffed at the time, but he was right…God has brought me much further than I ever dreamed. This is not to imply, in any way, that I have arrived. I am very much a continual work-in-progress. But like all God's followers, I am in the process of being perfected as He shapes me to become more and more like His Son, Jesus Christ.

My prayer is that my story will offer hope to rebels out there resisting and refusing a relationship with God. The very God you have turned your back on, is the same God who is offering you His hand, offering everything you've ever longed and searched for.

There was a time I thought I was too far gone…even for God. I was wrong. The fact that you're reading this means your heart is still beating, and your lungs still fill with air. And that means you too, still have a chance. Are you ready to leave behind familiar dark places and blaze new trails with God? Will you unclench your fist, and place your hand in God's now?

I don't know how your story will turn out…but from personal experience I can assure you that God's plans are much bigger and more satisfying than your own. Don't take my word for it, find out for yourself.

Rebel against the forces pushing you down a path that leads you to darkness and destruction, and embrace God as He leads you down a path that leads to light and life.

Bill LaMorey

IX

The Convict

Cleveland Bell

Shepherd's Song of Freedom

I was born in Thomasville, Georgia to Willie Mae and Cleveland Bell, Jr., the eldest of six brothers and sisters. In the South, racism is a fact of life--and growing up, I always had a real rough time accepting it. My genuine love for all people always made me feel different from my friends and the small world we lived in. It was made clear to me, on a daily basis, not everyone shared my outlook. And as a black man living south of the Mason-Dixon line, my viewpoint wasn't too important anyway.

According to the accepted double standards of that time, a black person was required to knock on the back door of a white person's home before he would be allowed entry. For some reason, delivering fish to a customer's home one day, I decided to go against those old school 'Jim Crow' social rules just to see what would happen.

Years earlier, I asked my Mom, "Why do we have to knock on the back door of white people's homes?" She told me, "That's just the way it is; that's the way it's always been."

"That's just the way it's always been?" I said to myself, "Well, that just doesn't cut it. I'm not goin' for that." My thoughts were righteous but I was ahead of my time. So, feeling ten feet tall and bullet proof, I went ahead and knocked on the customer's front door. I was thunderstruck when the customer whipped open the door yelling, "Nigger, if you don't get your ass to the back door, I'm gonna kick it everywhere but loose!"

Looking back, it seems that day marked the beginning of my life taking a downward spiral. I was 18 when my family packed up and left racist, small-town America for the "good life" in the big city--Miami.

Instead of the opportunity my parents hoped for, Miami turned into a mountain of irresistible temptation and seduction for me. Almost immediately after we settled in, my goal became to make it big in the nightclubs. I wanted to be part of the action. I was content to start at the bottom, taking a job as a pot washer at a club called Burdine's. When the joint closed, I began trying to live the after-hours 'cool' scene which included experimenting with weed.

I guess I was willing to believe that drugs were part of big city life and, of course, it wasn't long before my drug use escalated to "the heavier the better." I tried amphetamines, speed, LSD...I even mainlined paregoric with an opium base...the whole nine yards. I remember taking LSD one night and getting so high I thought I had the power to fly. Leaping out of a fifth story window to prove my newfound super power seemed like a good idea. A friend jerked me back into the room just before my feet left the ledge.

You'd think that would've set me straight, but I was too blind to be scared away from the drug life. It's almost like I had something to prove. Then, hanging out at a drug dealer's house, I met a 16-year old girl and got her pregnant. My foggy sense of right and wrong told me that the right thing to do was marry a woman if I got her pregnant; so I did. But, six years of marriage and two children later, we were a lot farther apart than together, in every possible way. I still wanted to hang out, hit the clubs, sell drugs; I wanted my cake and eat it too. After two more kids and some hard and truly painful times, we caved in and divorced.

Of course I was pretty depressed about the breakup. My genius solution? ... I got drunk and enlisted in the army. Boom... you talk about a lifestyle shock?!?! The army served as a mixed blessing for me. For the first time in my life, I was placed in a disciplined, structured environment where I was required to submit to authority. This was exactly the structure I needed to mature and, in the Army; I discovered something I had never known. I had the capability to do things well on my own.

However, the army served as my personal conduit for more drug use. Serving in Korea, I "dabbled" in drugs ("dabbling" is drug use, but not on a scale that could be labeled addiction) but didn't become truly addicted until I returned to Florida. It was there that I overdosed. My heart actually stopped beating. When I came to, my head was in the lap of a friend. I don't know how he got my heart beating again, but we were both drenched in sweat. Even my second severe brush with death didn't wake me up; it just made me more careful. By the time I was released from the army, getting high, brawling, stealing, avoiding responsibility, and covering up had become my normal way of life.

Once again, I was strung out; stoned and nodding out in the seedy lobby of another cheap hotel, I heard a faint but familiar voice calling, "Get up Poppa. Wake up. It's time to go home." It was my mother. Ever since I was a boy, my mother always called me Poppa because I was the man of the house. She poured me into a car, brought me home, and gave me all the TLC I needed to get back on the good foot. To show her my appreciation, I stole every dime she had and anything pawnable I could carry. I went right back to the low-down street life with a vengeance. My predictable and vicious cycle continued. Then I took it to the next phase of self-destruction. Now I was shooting up speed, weighing in at a whopping 100 pounds…a ghost of my former self.

I had lowered myself to purse-snatching to get drug money. One day, in broad daylight, I was trying to pull a purse from a lady's shoulder. I was so weak, I couldn't even pull it from her grip. I just hung there in desperation. It finally dawned on me that I had really hit the bottom. Where was my life? Where was my strength? I had been trained as a soldier to kill people, and now I couldn't even lift the weight of a lipstick, a compact, and a few credit cards.

When the squad car rolled up and they surveyed the situation, one of the uniforms said, "Let's take this nigger over by that abandoned warehouse and put him out of his misery." At that point, my "black man-in-a-white man's world" fear kicked in and I fully expected a merciless beating or worse. But instead, the metro police handed me over to the army MP's. I was charged with attempted robbery, possession of narcotics, and sentenced to five years of military jail time.

That sentence was the best thing that ever happened to me.

I was given plenty of time to think in that stockade. I began to realize that my addictions and my petty crimes were never my intentional choice. The drugs and the stealing served as some kind of counterfeit quick-fix for the acceptance, love, and belonging I never found. I was alone.

So out of pure boredom, I began reading the Bible. The words began to transform my mind and change my heart. I began to see that Jesus understood my struggles and me.

Jesus, while he was here on earth, was spit on, despised, distrusted, betrayed by his friends, and forced to prove himself at every turn. Growing up a black man, deep in the racist South, it seemed to me that Jesus and I had a lot in common. Jesus was tempted in every way but, unlike me, He was without sin. But relating to him as a character in a book was about as far as I took it. I still yearned for the comfort zone of my old lifestyle: drugs, women, and more drugs.

It was just another day, serving one more day of time, when I saw several other convicts coming out of the chapel room, heads hung low and actually crying. My head was still so twisted, that my first thought was, "Wow, they must have some really dynamite dope in there!" And if they had dope in there, I was definitely going in to check it out. Of course there was no dope inside. Instead there was a just a man speaking ... standing before another small group of cons. Jerry Raskin was a former addict turned evangelist. He was sharing his heartfelt testimony with each convict who came into that chapel. Before I joined the audience I gave the room another 'once-over,' still looking for hidden dope.

To this day, I don't know what made me decide to go along with accepting what was happening at that moment, in that room. But that was the day I let Jesus into my heart. I found myself on my knees praying and wondering if Jerry would ever stop testifying. Man, that guy could talk forever. Then, something happened. It felt like a giant boulder was being lifted off my chest. I knew I was feeling the presence of God. He was right there *with* me. I realized that I would never again have to carry my burdens alone. Then, out of nowhere, I started speaking at warp speed in a language I didn't know and had never heard.

The whole thing really shook me up and when I returned to my cell and tried to tell the guys what had happened, they just laughed. But, when I started to speak, a gradual hush came over the cells around me. Hearing my words, some extremely tough men broke down and wept. This was my confirmation that what took place in that chapel room, that day, was for real.

With God on my side, I thought I would surely be able to get released from prison early, but that wasn't God's plan. His plan for me was to serve out the full length of my sentence. Being refused release provided me more time to think and study. I attended a Bible-Study taught by Reverend Denver Smoot, also head of the drug-rehabilitation program called Turning Point. I enrolled in a Bible study correspondence course through the Billy Graham Evangelist Association. And by the time I was released from prison, I was well grounded in my faith.

Two years after I got out of jail, God blessed me with my wife Cindy, and good things began to happen as I started to consistently let God run my life. I was afraid to succeed, though, fearing failure more than craving success. But eventually, I applied to Miami Dade Community College and struggled through my first semester in every way imaginable. But with help and support from friends, I barely made it. Starting with the next semester, I continuously made the Dean's Honor Roll. I transferred to Florida International University and graduated with a B. A. in music and began finding my talent as a singer. It was almost impossible for me to believe that an ex-convict, ex-thief, ex-drug addict like myself could make such a turnaround.

"I can do <u>everything</u> through Him who gives me strength?" (Philippians 4:13)

A prominent Miami builder and brother in Christ, Charles Babcock, asked me if I would teach a Bible study at Riverside House, a halfway house for ex-offenders. Honestly, I didn't want the job. I argued with God. "Lord," I said, "You've blessed me with this big, strong voice and I just know you want the world to hear it. Just get me on the Johnny Carson show and I'll take it from there!"

God responded, "Cleve, where did I find you?"

I protested and said, "But Lord, the church would get 10% of a hundred thousand dollars! Think of all the Bibles that would buy!" ... There's a reason I was called a convict...I was still trying to con. But I realized God couldn't be conned, and I accepted the offer to help out at Riverside House—the halfway house for ex-offenders.

So instead of pursuing a career in show business, every Tuesday night found me leading a Bible study at Riverside House. After a year, the Executive Director took a sabbatical, and I was asked to fill in for him until he returned. Nearly thirty-five years later, I'm still waiting for the replacement.

Becoming Executive Director of a halfway house was not only the farthest thing from my mind, but was something I never dreamed would occur...I thought my calling was to be a singer. But the best plan is His plan—it's just a little hard to read His blueprint sometimes.

The place was a dump. We had twelve clients and four staff members (myself, Burt Rosen, Ken Norell, and Noreen Norell). Therefore, the twelve clients became my crew, splitting twenty-four hour non-stop shifts. My wife and I worked twelve hour shifts. I would cook, drive the thrift store truck full of donated items, lead meetings, and fill in during midnight shifts when staff didn't show up. We did this for five years. We received much support from our home church, surrounding churches, and other faithful servants of Christ.

"Now to him who is able to do immeasurably more than all we ask or imagine, according to His power that is at work within us." (Ephesians 3:20)

But the biggest struggle was finding the money to pay our staff. Without a decent staff, there was no Riverside House. God used this challenge to keep us on our knees, and fully depend on Him. But despite the struggle, God was faithful, and always came through.

But in a way, I am a shepherd of sheep like me. Sheep, perhaps, that had a few loose screws like I did, and sheep that can be herded. But these sheep are a different species and you've got to teach and herd using unorthodox methods.

Drug tests for our residents were normal, but residents were professionals at finding loopholes in our testing system. So I developed my own version - a random, unannounced drug test for residents who I strongly suspected were using. With urine sample kit in hand, I'd inform them of their final opportunity to confess to taking drugs just before running the test. If a resident said nothing, I would go into another room, put soap on the rim of the sample, and shake it up. With the 'telltale' frothing sample in hand, I would come back to show the resident that his urine sample was dirty. The resident would always confess at that point. I was their shepherd…but sometimes I had to use unorthodox methods keep the flock safe from the wolves in the night.

But I wasn't always the best shepherd. I was so focused on making the facility work that I sometimes acted before I thought a situation through. I would fire people on the spot, only to realize I was acting like a sheep, not a shepherd. God's grace helped me to use my errors and change my heart.

If there's one thing I love most about God; it's His way of recycling people. I'm convinced that "God doesn't make junk." He can't make junk. I've seen life examples of this truth by observing the ex-offenders at Riverside House as well as recalling my own pot-holed journey. God shows how things from our past are not only for our good, but also for His glory.

I could hear God reminding me, "Cleve, you were a hungry beggar once and found bread. All you have to do is go and tell others beggars where that bread is."

Today, Riverside House is an accredited 110 bed residential facility serving men, women, and substance abusers. But I dream big for the Lord. No longer do I fear success. If it's His will, I see Riverside Houses taking different shapes, and healing more. And maybe someday that replacement will come and let me retire, but I'm not holding my breath.

And even though I never made it to the Tonight Show, my naive dreams of recognition have been fulfilled in many ways. I sometimes fill in as Chaplin for the Miami Heat, Pittsburgh Steelers, or Miami Dolphins. I've been the given the opportunity to testify in Congress on rehabilitation, and you may have seen me on national TV singing the National Anthem at a Miami Dolphins game.

But my message is simple. I once was lost, but now am found. He saved a wretch like me because I said OK God…now I'm ready.

CLEVELAND BELL III

X

The Executive

Mark Hughes

For the Love of Money

Money........the mean green.......the almighty dollar. Looking back, I clearly see a time in my life when I loved money even more than I loved my wife and children.

I was enraptured by it, motivated by it, and I measured my success by it. My life plan was simple: Make as much money as possible, as fast as possible.

As a young executive, I quickly worked my way up the PepsiCo corporate ladder, and was known as a take no prisoners, "fire-in-the-belly" kind of guy. However, my bosses told me my potential to enter the exalted senior executive status was limited without the all-important initials, MBA, after my name. So within a year, I enrolled in one of the country's Top Ten Business Schools. I closely followed the strategy of every "How to" book ever written; setting definite goals and wasting no time hitting them, one after another.

At 34, I became one of the youngest officers of a publicly traded billion-dollar company. I was a marketing executive ruling a $40 million budget, using the same ad agency as Budweiser. I had a staff of 30 people, and I knew how to optimize millions of dollars of advertising with sophisticated analyses. But I had no idea how to successfully manage people. I was a smart guy...just not a warm guy.

I was ripe to make a career shift, and the timing for my move couldn't have been more perfect. I left the billion-dollar corporation for a small start-up named half.com. As its Marketing VP, I literally put the brand on the map by audaciously renaming the town of Halfway, Oregon to...Half.com, Oregon. My idea to change the town's name paid off big. Only 19 days after the official name change, eBay got interested in buying our company. **Time magazine** called it "one of the greatest publicity coups" in history. We sold the company to eBay for $312 million in just a matter of months.

Things were good. But my severe lack of people skills regularly held me back. You'd think people would've lined up in the rain to work for a guy who put a brand on the map that sold for $300+ million. But I discovered the exact opposite--people were actually ready to quit because of me. It served as my first real wake-up call.

The truth hurts, and the truth was--I sucked as a leader. I had bought into the quintessential smart-ass syndrome. I thought I was cooler than ice with my Columbia MBA and my Fortune 50 resume. The fact that people wouldn't follow me and were put off by the idea of ever doing so was alarming. All of my plans to carve out a successful future were definitely being threatened, by no one else but me.

I was far too proud to ask advice from any of my colleagues. The only person I felt I could turn to for help was my wife. I had met Kathy at PepsiCo when she was another of their "rising stars." Her fast track up the corporate totem pole was even faster than mine. Her peer reviews and management evaluations ranked tops among executives across all of PepsiCo's divisions, *globally*.

Briefly putting aside my larger-than-large ego, I laid it out for her; describing how people were ready to quit the company because of me. I confided to her that I had no idea how to begin fixing the problem, and that I was dying to know what her secret was. My wife turned to me, at the kitchen table and asked, "When you talk to your people, do you ask them about their lives, their wives, girlfriends or what they did over the weekend?"

I answered, "No. Why would I do that? When I need numbers or data, that's all I need and that's all I ask for."

She paraphrased my answer for me slowly saying, "Let me get

this straight. You don't talk to your employees about what's going on in their lives…it's all about business?"

"Of course, nothing but the bottom line," I replied. And that's when she, as delicately as possible, explained what I'd been consistently blind to for my entire professional life; that I needed to have a genuine relationship with people who were working their asses off for me, day in and day out. She let me know that people need more than just a paycheck for the work they perform. I started to see the basic truth in her words. What I had thought of as my well-tailored, no frills, straight-forward, business style completely left out all human element; and I started right then and there to slowly develop a genuine interest in the lives of my employees. In doing so I was also taking the first <u>tiny</u> step towards becoming a better person.

However, I was just touching the tip of the iceberg, as far as dealing with the depth of my self-absorption. I was going to have to deal with problems that lay far beyond my business relationships. My family and my friends were living with a completely driven and self-centered workaholic. If they weren't directly involved in my shortsighted, monetary goals, I would leave them on the outside looking in. They say that rationalization can be a fatal addiction, and I had it so wrong that I was convinced my family would benefit from this possessed "dedication" in the long run. With my ego at full tilt, I had become a virtual stranger to those who loved me.

Today, I realize I possessed a massive amount of fear. Even though I had built my savings to a very comfortable size, I was petrified that at any moment it would all be gone and I would be left destitute. In my mind, a financial doomsday was right around every corner and there was nothing I could do to stop it. I was convinced that I had to be in charge 24/7 to keep my boat from sinking.

My control issues started young. When I was three years old, my family lived in Hong Kong while my father covered the Vietnam War and Asia as a journalist.

One weekend, my parents took me on a sailboat trip in the bay of the South China Sea with two other families. I wanted to be like the big kids who weren't wearing life preservers. My parents had warned me of the dangers of not wearing one, but I threw a fit to get my way and my parents caved in. The verdict was: No life preserver for the strong-headed three-year-old.

Then, as I was walking along the side of this 30-foot Chinese junk, with one hand holding a dinner plate and the other holding a handrail, a wave rocked the boat. My head shot forward hitting the rail, knocking the front tooth out. I fell into the South China Sea, unconscious. And began my descent.

It was dark—just past dusk. One man heard a splash, dove in, found me sinking, and pulled me back up. He was in the right place at the right time; if he hadn't been there a three-year-old boy would have died. I thought I knew best, but it was God that had a plan to save me. Why? I've since come to understand that the one looking out for that willful knucklehead was God--the very same God I had been strongly pushing away my whole life.

A Man Named 'E'

At the age of 42, I thought I was fairly successful. I had the all the generally accepted requirements to live 'the good life.' I just had a book on marketing released by the second largest publisher in the world. I was being paid $15,000 per engagement to speak about my business practices. I had a healthy savings account and was driving the obligatory BMW. I had started down the right road to give people that worked with me and for me, the respect they deserved. I had deleted "smart-ass" from my personality menu. But in my home, the place requiring the most care and attention, I was a dumb-ass.

When I entered my home at night, I was a human landmine, ready to explode at any moment.

When simple around-the-house projects went wrong, I would roar at the top of my lungs, "Jesus F--ing Christ!!!!!" When my toddler son acted up, as toddlers often do, I had absolutely no patience with him and would lose it completely.

As long as my image had anything to do with my business, I could be Mr. Cool.

But at night or on the weekends, I would explode when anything got tense, frustrating, or difficult. I was not easy to live with.

I was constantly hunting for business, because there was never enough money to keep me from being nervous about the future. I reached out to an acquaintance from several years back. He too, had a track record of business success, but greater than mine. I emailed him, and we began to reconnect. I was dabbling with an upcoming TV venture, and my friend 'E' had invested in a feature film with A-list stars ("The Mighty Macs"), and invited me to the shoot on his set.

On the back-lot, he asked if I would devote some free time to a new company he bankrolled. My 'to cool for school' businessman synapses clicked in and thought to myself, "I get 15 grand per speech and I'm going to do this for nothing? This guy must be out of his mind!"

But perhaps for the first time in my life, a stronger voice in the back of my head whispered loudly, *"Just shut up and do it."*

A couple of weeks later 'E' asked, "Can we meet *every* week?" I was a little upset at the growing time commitment...but I said OK. The more I got to know 'E', the more I wanted to be around him. He was solid, successful, grounded, and had an amazing zest for life. There was something about him.

But one morning, 'E' asked me, "Hey Mark I never thought to ask you, but at 7:30 am every Friday we have a men's Gospel reflection. I don't know where you are in your faith, but we'd certainly like to have you come by and check it out."

42 years of turmoil flashed before me.

I was raised as a Christian Scientist. At 12, I began to question many things that were inherent to that religion. Christian Scientists didn't believe in matter. For example, they would be quick to inform you that the book you're reading right now isn't real. The chair you're sitting on isn't real.

I would ask, "If this chair isn't real, why haven't I fallen off and landed on my ass?!? The pat answer given was: "The *idea* of the chair is real, but the chair itself is not real." I would ask about the soldiers on TV getting killed. The answer again was that anything made of matter (such as the human body) is not real and therefore can't be killed. I've always respected the right to practice many belief systems that don't cause harm, but the pragmatic side of my brain just couldn't buy it.

For me, all organized religion was loaded with inconsistencies and all my frustrations and questions came rushing back.

I believed in God, and definitely believed in destiny. In the back of my mind, I thought that, somewhere down the road, I would embrace some religious concept; perhaps Buddhism, Judaism, or something else. I wasn't sure, but I knew there had to be some belief system out there with my name on it. So I answered my friend 'E' saying, "So far, in my life, I haven't been much of a religious person, but I think my faith could be increasing."

Maybe it was my need to find release from what was gnawing at my insides. I knew that beyond the workplace, my life and my reactions to life were as dysfunctional as you could get. I mean how many times could I yell at my wife and precious children? How many times could I scream, "Jesus F--ing Christ" whenever the slightest thing went wrong? How many more times could I let my need to be in charge take over my every reaction? I was drowning on dry land.

But maybe there was a way out. Maybe my time to find that way was now.

The very next Friday morning, I woke up early and scrambled out the door to the 7:30 am meeting. I didn't tell my wife. I didn't tell anyone. If this thing didn't work out, or if I was greeted by a bunch of half-crazed Holy Rollers, I could always pretend it never happened. I was terrified. But the door was opening. I wasn't sure if that door would be a dead-end, be slammed in my face, or be the door that my heart knew would open someday.

There were twenty men assembled at a long table that morning. Just average working men…building contractors, marines, dentists, and businessmen. Some confessed to being former alcoholics, some had been deeply involved with drugs over the years. But very quickly I observed that none of their past lives mattered to the morning's purpose. Two prayers were read (the Litany of Humility, and the Prayer of Pope Clement) and then the Gospel (which is the Catholic Church's most important Sunday passage). I had always thought of Gospel as a genre of music, and this was as foreign to me as Chinese arithmetic. After the passage was read there was deafening silence.

Twenty men, completely silent...it seemed like the stillness would last forever.

I looked around. Some men had their eyes closed. Some just stared at the table...almost through the table. One-by-one, they began to share what the reading meant to them. Some said they had difficulty understanding what a particular sentence meant. Other men would digress, sharing very personal, and sometimes overly personal experiences. Men were sharing things that "real men" just didn't share.

I said nothing. I was scared to death.

There were some more prayers said at the end – none of which I was familiar with. Something about 'Mary full of grace.' Later my friend 'E' pulled me aside to make sure I was OK, and asked me how I liked the meeting. I told him it had been slightly nerve-wracking for me, but that I liked what a guy named Joe had said. And then I heard myself telling him that I was interested enough to return the following Friday to learn more.

My definition of 'more' had always been money. But I was starting to wake up to the fact that there had to be something besides the acquisition of money...something bigger than my plans...something that had meaning for the rest of my life. I had no idea what it was, but I felt ready for the exploration.

The Power of Words

Around the same time I was attending my first 'Gospel Reflection' meeting, I began reading a book called "Success Principles" by Jack Canfield (he was on the Board of one of my clients). I read the section that basically said every successful person had to understand their life's purpose. That was going to be a major stumbling block for me since, as far as I could tell, I had no life purpose: none. Making money isn't a purpose; it was a function... as necessary as going to the bathroom.

I had built my entire career on the foundation of an Ivy League MBA, a Fortune 50 resume, and a marketing book published in 14 languages, only to find that I had no foundation at all.

After reading this book, my friend 'E' turned me on to another book almost by accident. In 'E's office, there was a guy who'd gotten married six months earlier. 'E' said to him, like he was talking to a kid brother, "six months of marriage and your honeymoon's about over. You're gonna need to read this book. But you might not have the cojones for it."

Sitting nearby, I said, "What's this book?"

"Discovering the Mind of a Woman, by Ken Nair." He told me the same thing, "Read it only if you've got the cojones."

He was challenging my manhood. I told him, "I'll read the book."

In a few days I began reading. As I poured over each page of "Discovering the Mind of a Woman," I was horrified. It was a near mirror image of my life, which went like this:

I work my ass off every day to try and provide.

My wife gives me a hard time about not spending enough time with the family.

I'm working!

I'm nervous about the future... and I continue to work harder.

My wife continues to nag more.

It seems like she's nagging all the time.

And sex. What happened? We used to do it once (sometimes twice) a day.

She's not satisfying me with what a man needs... once a week, or once every two or three weeks!

I try and talk to her and she's not listening... more nagging.

Now when I come home, I simply retreat.

I work my ass off for 11 hours, am facing a terrible boss, and who knows what's going to happen at work. But I don't show my fear, because I don't want to cause her alarm.

And on top of this crap, I'm not getting love from my wife.

The only way I can relax and release worry is if I retreat on my own.

Sooner than later, you retreat from your family--in your own house.

And sooner than later, your wife sees you retreating.

And one day you notice, not only is your physical relationship nearly gone, your relationship in general pretty much sucks.

When was the last time you talked to your wife…asked her about her life?

When did she ask you about your hopes and dreams?

And both of you begin to grow apart.

Perhaps with other added complications: medical problems, a layoff, a release which turns into an addiction, and more complications.

While reading, I saw my past and future flash before me. I had barely dodged divorce twice already with my wife, but after reading this book I knew I was still behaving like an outright ass to my wife and children on a daily basis. The haunting similarity to my life in Nair's words served as another loud wake-up call.

I identified with the author, because he talked about his very dominating and selfish drive for sex, confessing thoughts like, "I think I'd like to have sex with my wife. I should wake her up and roll her over now." His admissions were duplicates of my daily thoughts and feelings. I couldn't really identify with the imposing image of Jesus's perfection; but Nair was completely relatable because, like me, he was flawed in so many ways. He was presenting a mirror for me to see an accurate image of my life…and I definitely didn't like what I saw.

A major change had to be made. I began at home with my kids, making solid efforts to be more patient than I ever had. I resisted the urge to blurt out "Jesus Christ," let alone "Jesus F--king Christ" whenever I was frustrated. I began trying to communicate with my wife in a meaningful way, knowing it would involve continual effort and plain old hard work, more than anything I had ever attempted. And, I'm trying to accept the fact that my road in the right direction is long, and on most days I probably fall short.

Fortunately, I was given a chance to make things better before they got worse. I continued showing up every Friday morning to the Gospel reflection discussion, discovering stories that were new to me, like "The Prodigal Son" and "The Good Shepherd." Every week, I was able to learn a lot about myself as those twenty stalwart men shared the sometimes heart-wrenching stories of their past and present lives.

Another Step

A routine business meeting brought me in contact with a former associate, Steve, who had since become a pastor. I told him about my new journey, and how excited I was to be taking my first steps. I told him about the two books that had impressed me so far, and asked him what books he was reading? He paused and asked me in a serious tone, "Mark, those sound like great books, but have you read the Bible?"

Semi-stunned by his sudden mood change, I said, "Uhh, nope. I haven't yet." Steve's response made me feel like a kid on the way to school without his homework: "If you ever arrive at the gates of heaven to be judged…how can you possibly expect to have a shot at entry without having read the word of God?" He continued, "Tell you what, Mark; if you're serious about this journey you've started, you need to get a Bible, and start reading the New Testament. Start there for now."

I didn't even own a Bible. I went home, got online, and charged seven dollars to my credit card. Two days later an unopened bible arrived at my front door. Man, it was difficult reading. I had no clue what was going on. The font was so small, and the language so awkward. But I followed Steve's advice, because he was the kind of guy who always had it together, a guy who always exceeded his financial targets (which obviously got my immediate attention and respect), got promoted fast, and got stuff *done*. He was the executive you just loved to be around. He had that same special quality as my friend 'E'. So I kept at it, and continued to read the New Testament.

When Steve mentioned "heaven" I realized that I had no idea about what heaven was or how I could even remotely relate to it.

What was heaven? One of the men in our Friday Gospel reflection group recommended a book that he said was inspirational for him. Reading "90 Minutes in Heaven" was the next big step in my journey. It was written by a man named Don Piper who had "officially" been declared dead for 90 minutes after a head-on collision with an 18-wheel tractor-trailer. Four sets of paramedics took his pulse, checked for breathing, and pronounced him dead at the scene, leaving him in his mangled car. 90 minutes later, a priest who'd gotten into the car to pray for him, felt him move, and called a paramedic over for help. The paramedic told him, "He's dead."

But the fact was, he was still alive... and the book details what the author saw for those 90 minutes. The amazing colors, the gates, the incredible sounds, and the peace. And then, his return back to earth.

There is a heaven. I might not have ever experienced it, but Don Piper's story left me with little doubt. The Bible's description of Heaven doesn't seem very articulate but Piper wrote in detail about his journey there and what he saw and felt. I could visualize his every reaction. For the first time in my life, I had faith. Something I never personally experienced... something I never physically touched... but something I believed in. However, I didn't want to completely abandon a practical approach to investigation.

I remember a scientist, being interviewed on a television documentary, making an analogy that stuck in my mind: "I've never been to Tokyo, so how would I know that Tokyo *really* exists? To believe Tokyo really exists, you combine reason with faith." At this point in my learning, this was what I was doing... combining reason with faith.

I kept my Bible reading going, almost like doing push-ups – beneficial drudgery, but at this stage it was my three newly discovered reads by Canfield, Nair, and Piper that were truly rocking my world. It was almost like a customized "Faith for Dummies" trilogy, matched seamlessly with my lack of formal religious training.

"We need to ask ourselves a question… are we human beings living a spiritual existence, or spiritual beings living a human existence?"

This was the basic question/premise introduced in "Embraced by the Light," another book brought up for discussion in one of our Friday morning meetings. I'm sure that the author, Betty Eadie, had no idea her work would be another personal and instrumental key for me to unlock the door to all that I needed and now yearned to understand. Of course, that question will always instigate hours of heated debate among sophisticated and would-be philosophers in any room. What is the answer? It was like the parable, "If a tree falls in the forest and nobody hears it fall… does it make a sound?" I didn't know the answer, but I would soon find out.

A few weeks later, my 84 year-old uncle's health had taken a turn for the worse. Death was imminent. Uncle Dick had smoked like a chimney since his early teens and now was paying for that "pleasure" by having to deal with COPD. He was going down quickly and, that week, was moved into a hospice facility. Just like most people, I'd been afraid of death my whole life. Perhaps I developed a super-sized fear from my near drowning in Hong Kong all those years ago.

I had just finished "Embraced by the Light," right before I left to be with my Uncle and his wife. The words in that book gave me my first real understanding of what death was all about. Understanding the concept made my fear completely disappear. The author, Betty Eadie, writes about her own death, going to heaven, and her eventual return. In her case, she died at four and then again at 31. She describes heaven, meeting Jesus, the sounds, the colors, and how a virtual video of her life seemed to play before her. She was able to see the ripple effect of the good things from her life, as well as the bad -- affecting friends, relatives, and strangers alike throughout the ripple.

It's clear she would have nothing to gain by telling her story and subjecting herself to ridicule, but here again (like knowing that Tokyo exists without having been there), you have to combine faith and reason to decide, in your own heart, what is true. I wasn't sure of everything I had read in the Bible; but after reading her book, I believed in Heaven as surely as I believed in Tokyo. She also believed in satan, describing him in detail in the book...and this was another shock to me. The layers of the onion just kept getting peeled back.

As far as I was concerned, the concept of satan was just great fuel for fairy tales and bad dreams for seven-year olds. I thought satan was as grounded in reality as Santa Claus. But if there is an ultimate force of evil in this world, Eadie's description of a plausible power of darkness made sense. She saw the posse of satan, literally, as they tried to corral her, only to be chased away by guardian angels.

Ever since reading "Embraced by the Light," I've firmly believed that satan exists. Keep in mind that up to that point, my skeptical quotient for religion was pretty darn high. I didn't accept anything at face value.

Reading this book before my Uncle died finally gave me complete peace and understanding (the true definition of closure) with death. I didn't fear his death. I was honored that he asked me to be there with him during his final moments of life. As I stood by his bedside, looking out the window of his room, I caught a glimpse of the beauty and peace that was waiting ahead of him. The day he died, I gave his wife "Embraced by the Light."

The Friday morning meetings seemed to fly by. I was finally beginning to connect the dots between the New Testament and the everyday, and not so everyday, struggles that the men were describing in vivid detail. I was surprised when 'E' missed a couple of Fridays in a row, but was told that he was traveling in Israel on a last minute trip with a fellow Christian businessman. When he got back, he told our group that, in his opinion, visiting and exploring Israel was essential for anybody wanting to know more about God. Two months later, my speaking agent called to let me know I might have a gig coming up in Tel Aviv, Israel. My immediate response was, "Don't negotiate on price, just book it."

As soon as my plane touched down in Tel Aviv I immediately connected with a colleague of a Holy Land guide I had researched online. Christopher Cross (yes, it's his real name: www.catholicholyland.com).

I was taken to the most Holy places in all of Christianity for the next three days. My jaw was on the ground, being able to see and touch living history. I threw two books in my bag for the trip: the Holy Bible and "The Purpose Driven Life" by Rick Warren. I somehow found myself reading non-stop. Maybe it was the mood the ancient city put me in, but I just couldn't put the books down. My life's purpose came into sharp focus. "The Purpose Driven Life," speaks specifically about *serving*. "We are only here to serve." Rick Warren's take on serving is not 'helping serve the homeless in the soup kitchen during holidays for charity' variety. He was speaking of, as he phrased it, "the three T's": giving your *time*, your *treasure*, and your *talents*.

Did I really have to travel halfway around the world to commit myself to read all of Matthew, Mark, Luke, and John? Perhaps to begin breaking through my thick head. It was awe-inspiring to read a passage from the Bible one day, and the very next day go stand where the story actually happened. It was real...I walked the very paths and touched the very stones that Jesus touched.

But for whatever reason, many of the Bible's concepts still weren't getting through to me. One morning my guide took me to the birthplace of John the Baptist. He said, "You know the story of John being born, and his father becoming mute, right?"

Still falling prey to a bit of pride I said, "Why don't you refresh my memory."

Twenty minutes later we were at the spot where Mary visited Elizabeth when John leaped in her womb. My guide said, "You know the story of the visitation, right?"

"Uhh, can you retell it for me?"

It was perhaps one of the most seminal moments in the Bible where Mary's cousin Elizabeth, pregnant well beyond her childbearing years with John the Baptist, was visited by the young

Mary. It is said that John, inside Elizabeth's womb, leapt in the direction of Mary, who was pregnant with Jesus.

Incredible!! I read the very words in Luke the night before, and it still didn't stick! How dumb was I? I had to learn the hard way -- by going to the actual scene of all these miraculous events. I guess my head had become thick from countless years as a nay-saying, wise-ass skeptic of anything religious.

◆ ◆ ◆

I once thought I knew where I was going. Full steam ahead, of course, following my plan. But I discovered my plan wasn't working so well. I had no sense of peace and no sense of purpose...until I gathered the strength to open a door in my heart and let God in.

Now, just as I believe in the existence of a place called Tokyo without ever having been in Tokyo, I now believe in God and his Word in the Bible. I also believe in the messages and stories told by regular people, flawed just like you and me. And I find strength in the kinship and knowledge I receive from twenty men every Friday morning.

Year after year I said "not now" to a feeling buried deep inside my soul. I was afraid. But now...now after understanding that there's a plan written for me by God, I know this to be true: The *less* faith I put in *my* plan and the *more* faith I put in *God's* plan... the more peace I experience. I now know that trying to make it on my own is a sure ticket to failure.

For 42 of my years on the planet, peace had been glaringly missing from my life. It was only after accepting God's unfolding plan (better late than never) that I started to experience the over-whelming, calming, and comforting sense of peace I had always yearned for.

The answers to every question and the way to attain peace, can only be found by letting go of our own plan. By combining faith with reason, and believing in God's plan...following God's plan.

Open the door. Yes, it's scary, and the path forward isn't well lit. But there is peace, and there is happiness.

Reach for that door inside you. Because if not now...when?

Mark Hughes

A parting note ...

A wise man once said, "A man is but the product of his thoughts. <u>What he thinks, he becomes</u>." Change your thinking, and you will begin to change your life. All of us (the ten contributors to this book) came to a crossroads where each of us had to make the same tough decision: choosing between dying a little more each day or changing in order to survive and grow. You've no doubt noticed the one similarity in all of our stories is that self-reliance fell short time and time again. We all dug ourselves into some pretty deep emotional holes. We had to learn, each in our own time, how to stop relying on our own ego. We all had to learn that with Jesus Christ as our guide, we would discover places we could never find on our own.

The pain and suffering incurred in our lives caused massive resentment in each of us. And that resentment instilled fear and loathing, which in turn caused our lives to take self-destructive turns. We were weighed down by lifelong grudges and the anxiety that naturally accompanies them. Eventually, each of us discovered *forgiveness* was the only way to lighten our heavy mental and emotional load. Forgiveness of those who wronged us along the way, intentionally or accidentally, and then forgiveness of ourselves--for all the collateral damage we inflicted on everyone in our previous path. This was the first step toward finding freedom and hope in our lives.

Many good men, making daily efforts to do the right thing, are shocked by the trials and hardships they run into along the highway of life. They shouldn't be, and we shouldn't be. Jesus actually *promised* we would have tribulations in our lives (read the book of Job in the Bible for a huge dose of tribulations given to one guy). But Jesus also promised us His presence to help us through those dark times.

Another thread of commonality that runs through all of our stories (our ten and yours): there is absolutely no way to predict where or when your 'now' moment will come...when you become just plain tired of bearing whatever burden you've been carrying, and you finally decide to reach out to a power greater than your own...and say, "Yes, I've said *not now* for my entire life, but I'm ready. Now, I'm ready."

And how is it for us today? Now that we've chosen to walk with God...is every day bright and sunny?...no. We know full well that sometimes things won't go our way. People will let us down. Circumstances seem to conspire to rip away our resolve to be better men. We may fail in our individual goals from time to time, and revert to negative thinking, which leads to bad decisions. The temptation to throw in the towel is undeniable and strong. But it is our sincere hope that you find inspiration in our stories...enough to dig further and take your first step toward freedom. As bad as your life ever seems to be, trust that God has a plan for you. Let Him be the one to lead, and the rest will take care of itself.

You are not alone on the journey. We are with you.

Ron Gruber
MICAH 7:7-9

Todd

Mike

Venela Boo

Bill

Mark

Tools for the Journey

I fail often but I shall try again.

When I rely on myself, I fail.

You are not the judge...there is only one judge.

Satan's biggest lie is tomorrow.

The Lord is my shepherd, I shall not want.

If you don't stand for something, you'll fall for anything.

You can focus on your problems, or focus on your purpose.

An eye for an eye makes the whole world blind - Ghandi

It is no longer I who lives, but Christ who lives in me - Saul

A man convinced against his will is of the same opinion still.

People pay more attention, to what you do than to what you say.

Courage is not the absence of fear, but moving forward with your fears.

We must try for joy in service, joy in suffering, and even joy in doubt.

For with God, nothing shall be impossible. Lk 1:37

If you're not part of the solution, you're part of the problem.

No success in business will compensate for failure at home.

Be quick to listen. Slow to speak.

What is the best religion? The one that brings you closer to God.

Beloved, do not trust every spirit but test the spirits to see whether they belong to God, because many false prophets have gone out into the world. Jhn 1, 4:1

World transformation begins with self-transformation.

All of theology comes down to one sentence: God gives, we blow it, and he forgives.

Keep your words sweet, because you never know when you might have to eat them later.

We don't have all the answers.

The only thing we can take with us is the good we have done to others. I saw that all of our good deeds and kind words will come back to bless us a hundredfold after this life. -Betty Eadie

I love my lord because he loved me first.

What we do here on earth is echoed in eternity.

God wants great things to happen to us, and He wants great things to happen through us.

Without struggle, there is no progress. –F. Douglass

You must make an investment...to get a return on investment.

If we can master gentleness, we can take a lot of hurt and keep working calmly. I keep thinking of the line in sports "You've got to learn to play hurt." Ok. We have to deal with our wounds responsibly, emotional or otherwise, but we have to stay in the holiness game while we do it. And that means seeing those we live with and work with as Jesus sees them and thus master the art of returning love for hostility. -Anne a lay apostle

In order to have a testimony, you have to be tested.

Every man has a king and a fool in him. The one you talk to is the one who responds to you.

If you wait to do everything until you're sure it's right, you'll probably never do much of anything.

Attitude is a little thing that makes a big difference. - Winston Churchill

When the student is ready, the teacher will appear.

More money won't change your life. A bigger house won't change your life. The only way to change your life is to change your habits. –Matthew Kelly, New York Times best selling author

Ten Books - knowledge for life's highway

Tough Times Never Last but Tough People Do - Robert Schueller

If you've ever been through a tough time or are in the thick of one now, this one's for you.

The Purpose Driven Life - Rick Warren

An easy read. The author sheds light on what we've been put here to do and accomplish in our lifetime.

How to Win Friends and Influence People - Dale Carnegie

Corny title, but this is a best-selling classic for a reason.

Discovering the Mind of a Woman - Ken Nair

If you're married, read it immediately. You might end up with more of what you always wanted.

The Greatest Salesman in the World - Og Mandino

Bad title… not about sales at all. Gather the wisdom of the ancients

My Descent Into Death - Howard Storm

If you don't think satan or hell exists, think again. This guy went to the dark side and came back.

Embraced by the Light - Betty Eadie

If you've ever had to deal with anyone close to you dying, read this. The first half is slow, but it gathers steam. You'll be glad you plowed through it.

Think and Grow Rich - Napoleon Hill

Hill profiles some of the richest men in the world and how their forward thinking drove their fortune, and more importantly provided them life-long richness of spirit.

Climbing the Mountain - Anne a lay apostle

Read this only after reading half the list. Written by a Chicago native now living in Ireland, who's been tapped by God in a special way. It's a true mind blower.

And, of course, the **Holy Bible** (starting with the New Testament)

Read Matthew, Mark, Luke, and John first...it's the ultimate history book.

Three Tunes – to keep a song in your heart

Lean On Me (Bill Withers)
Sometimes in our lives
We all have pain
We all have sorrow
But if we are wise
We know that there's
Always tomorrow

Lean on me
When you're not strong
I'll be your friend
I'll help you carry on
For it won't be long
Till I'm gonna need
Somebody to lean on

Please, swallow your pride
If I have things

You need to borrow
For no one can fill
Those of your needs
That you won't let show

You just call on me brother
When you need a hand
We all need somebody
To lean on
I just might have a problem
That you'll understand
We all need somebody to lean on

Lean on me
When you're not strong
I'll be your friend
I'll help you carry on
For, it won't be long
Till I'm gonna need
Somebody to lean on

You just call on me brother
When you need a hand
We all need somebody to lean on
I just might have a problem
That you'd understand
We all need somebody to lean on

If there is a load
You have to bare
That you can't carry
I'm right up the road
I'll share your load
If you just call me
Call Me
If you need a friend

(Call Me)
Call Me
If you need a friend
(Call Me)
If you ever need a friend
(Call Me)
Call Me
If you need a friend

Still Haven't Found What I'm Looking For (U2)
I have climbed highest mountains
I have run through the fields
Only to be with you
Only to be with you
I have run
I have crawled
I have scaled these city walls
These city walls
Only to be with you

But I still haven't found what I'm looking for
But I still haven't found what I'm looking for

I have kissed honey lips
Felt the healing in her fingertips
It burned like a fire
This burning desire

I have spoke with the tongue of angels
I have held the hand of a devil
It was warm in the night
I was cold as a stone

But I still haven't found what I'm looking for
But I still haven't found what I'm looking for

I believe in the Kingdom Come
Then all the colors will bleed into one
Bleed into one
But yes I'm still running

You broke the bonds
And you loosed the chains
Carried the cross
Of my shame
Oh my shame
You know I believe it

But I still haven't found what I'm looking for
But I still haven't found what I'm looking for
But I still haven't found what I'm looking for

A Change is Gonna Come (Sam Cooke)
I was born by the river in a little tent
Oh, just like the river, I been running ever since
It's been a long, a long time coming
But I know a change is gonna come
Oh, yes it will, look it here

It's been too hard living and I'm afraid to die
Look it here
Cuz I don't know what's up there beyond the sky
It's been a long
I wish I could come out there where you are baby
A long time coming but I know
Look it here
A change is gonna come, oh yes it will
Look it here

Let me say one more thing
I go to the movie and I go downtown
But I don't like it here

Somebody keep telling me oh boy, don't hang around
It's been a long, a long
If anybody know what I'm talking about
Lemme see you wave your hands
I know a chance gonna come, oh yes it will
But I gotta take, say this here

Then I go to my brother, yes sir
And I tell 'em, I say brother help me please
But he winds up knockin' me
He knocks me back down, back down on my
Oh there's been times that I fall
Somebody say yeah
Life could pass me on, no no
I know I'm able, I'm able, I'm able
I'm able to carry on
It's been a long, good God almighty
A long time coming but I know, yeah
A change is gonna come, oh yes it will
Look it here, one more time

Then I go to my brother
Somebody take your hands back and forth like this
Everybody, everybody
You sittin' in the first balcony too
All over the auditorium tonight
But he winds up knocking me down, my
Back down on, back down on my knee oh

I've been down but I thought I could last
Oh, I know I'm able, I'm able, I'm able
I know, I know, I know a change gonna come
And oh yes it will
Somebody say yeah
You all back here, lemme hear ya say yeah
Somebody say oh yeah

Somebody say oh yeah
Somebody say yeah
Whoa, right on

Three Prayers – to fuel your soul
Our Father, Who art in heaven
Hallowed be Thy Name;
Thy kingdom come,
Thy will be done,
on earth as it is in heaven.
Give us this day our daily bread,
and forgive us our trespasses,
as we forgive those who trespass against us;
and lead us not into temptation,
but deliver us from evil. Amen.

◆　◆　◆

Love is patient;
love is kind;
love is not envious or boastful or arrogant or rude.
It does not insist on its own way; it is not irritable or resentful;
it does not rejoice in wrongdoing, but rejoices in the truth.
It bears all things, believes all things, hopes all things, endures all
　　things.

◆　◆　◆

Dear God,
I have been saying not now to you all of my life, but I am ready.
I am a sinner; I have blown it like these ten men I just read about.
　　I don't deserve it, but I choose to accept your free gift of salva-
　　tion. Please forgive me of my sins, wash me clean and help me
　　to follow you all the days of my life.
Thank you for loving me and help me learn to love you back with
　　all of my heart.
I pray these things in the name of Jesus.

Find a Group Near You

Search online typing:

"Men's group" + my state (or town)

"Men's Bible study" + my state (or town)

Or, learn how to start your own men's group at
SonsofGrace.org/start